EDUCAT**I**ON
POLA**N**D

Past, Present, and Future

Kenneth R. Wulff

Kent State University

UNIVERSITY
PRESS OF
AMERICA

Lanham • New York • London

D1496330

Copyright © 1992 by
University Press of America®, Inc.
4720 Boston Way
Lanham, Maryland 20706

3 Henrietta Street
London WC2E 8LU England

Library of Congress Cataloging-in-Publication Data

Wulff, Kenneth R.
Education in Poland : past, present, and future /
Kenneth R. Wulff.
p.   cm.
Includes bibliographical references and index.
1. Education and state—Poland—History.   2. Education—
Poland—History—20th century.   3. Poland—History—1945–
I. Title.
LC93.P7W85   1992   379.438—dc20   92–4401 CIP

ISBN 0–8191–8614–7 (cloth : alk. paper)
ISBN 0–8191–8615–5 (pbk. : alk. paper)

To Joyce, Scott, Lori, and Karen, and to my Polish col-
leagues, who helped me so much.

EDUCATION IN POLAND: PAST, PRESENT AND FUTURE

TABLE OF CONTENTS

TABLES

FOREWORD

In this book Dr. Kenneth Wulff has surveyed a portion of Polish culture that is little known to American readers--its educational system. By concentrating on this one aspect he has provided valuable information on an aspect of the country that has focused so much attention of the world in recent years, during which Poland has played a pathbreaking role in the radical systematic changes in Eastern Europe that lead to the abandoning of totalitarian systems and entering the path toward democracy and political pluralism. It promises to be a long and difficult process and an element that will undoubtedly play a crucial role in it is going to be the educational system, both in the sense of its traditions and the new reforms just being introduced. Education has always played a central role in Poland's modern history; in the last two turbulent centuries, marked mostly by foreign occupations, it was the formal and informal education that had to undertake the task of preserving national identity and preparing for the future independence.

To any student of Polish history and culture it will be obvious that without some understanding of the educational system and its traditions an interpretation of the complex changes the country is now undergoing would be impossible.

Since the book centers on the post World War II educational system in Poland, it will be a useful aid for the reader who wishes to understand today the inheritance of the socialist system that has come to an end in 1990. Because of the rapidity of political transformation and relative slowness of systematic, structural change the book will also be valuable for those who wish to better acquaint themselves with some of the problems and needs that the new Poland is facing at present and in the future.

Michał J. Rozbicki
American Studies Center
Warsaw University

PREFACE

The swirl of events in contemporary Eastern Europe can mislead some observers into thinking that these developments are all spontaneous. In one country, at last, society has carefully prepared its citizens for this time of peaceful revolution. That country is Poland, and the preparation it has given its citizens, for better and for worse, is in its educational system.

This book examines the educational system of Poland, from the perspectives of the past, the present, and the future. As Norman Davies says in the preface to Heart of Europe: A Short History of Poland,(Davies 1989, vii) no book which sets out to relate the Past to the Present is ever written at the right moment. By the time the author's observations get out, the Present has moved on and becomes a part of the Past.

Davies' point applies here as material gathered during 1988-89 is used in the book. The author was on an academic year exchange at Warszawa University, Warszawa, Poland. Recent events in Eastern Europe and Poland in particular, highlight the need for such material to be available to readers. Very little material is available on Poland and virtually no material is available in the field of Education. The central purpose of this book, then, is to provide knowledge concerning education in Poland.

Therefore, Part I, examines The Past: Traditions. A brief historical background of education in Poland becomes the necessary base for the present. Part II provides current information on the Organization and Structure of the Educational System in Poland. Important topics include Management and Finance, structure of the present system of education, Teachers and Teacher Training, Parent views, and additional general information.

The author wants the reader to receive a balanced view of education in Poland. Therefore, Part III, The Future, builds on images of the past and images of the present to examine desired images in the future. During 1989, the Expert Committee for National Education issued a report. The two year study's major tasks were to diagnose the scope of the current Polish educational system and then to elaborate three future outlines which could allow for reform.

Without the help of many people in Poland, this book would not have been possible. Thanks and acknow-

PREFACE

ledgments are necessary to several Poles. The Polish
Teachers Association and Solidarity education leaders
were of special help. Warsaw University's Department
of Pedagogy, Dean Irena Szybiak, was especially useful
in securing information on the structure, management
and finance of Polish education. Prof. dr. hab. Cze
sław Kupisiewicz, Chair of the Presidium of the
Expert Committee, was kind to share reports of the
committee. The American Studies Center Director Michał Rozbicki, provided physical and spiritual help.
A word of personal appreciation goes to students in the
education course I taught and students in my wife's
conversational English class. Krzysztof Kruszewski, a
former Minister of Education provided much useful
information and became a good friend in the process.
Dr. Stefan Mieszalska, Chair of General Theory of
Instruction, Department of Education of the Warszawa
University, willingly secured many resources and pa-
tiently read the manuscript providing many needed
corrections.

"I don't understand how a serious writer these
days can judge his own terrain if he knows no
other."(Michener 1988, 669) It is the author's hope
that his readers will better understand and appreciate
their own educational terrain as a result of exposure
to another terrain.

MAP OF POLAND

POLAND

CHAPTER 1

INTRODUCTION

Official Name: Polish People's Republic - 1944-1990
                 The Republic of Poland - since 1990

Area: 120,756 Total area in square miles; 312,683
        Square kilometers:
        Slightly smaller than New Mexico (121,335
        square miles)

Capital: Warszawa (Warsaw)
           1,659,400 population

Population: 37,236,000 current population

             314 Population per square mile
             100 Population "doubling time" in years
             (at current rate)
             38,269,000 Population estimate 1989
             35,610,450 Population in 1978 census
             39,900,000 Population projected to year
             2000
             42,400,000 Population projected to year
             2020
             26%/9% (Percent of total population)
             Percent of population under age 15/over
             age 64
             61% Urban population
             39% Country/rural population

National   Minorities: Lithuanian;   White   Russian;
                         Ukrainian; Jewish; Czechoslo-
                         vak; Tartar; German; Mazur;
                         Karaim; Kusubian

Geography: The six major regions are 1) Pojezierze
             Pomorskie;
             2) Pojezierze Mazurskie; 3) Wielkopolska;
             4) Nizina Slaska;
             5) Malopolská; 6) Mazowsze

Political divisions: 49   Wojewodztwa (states)

                            804   Miasta (cities)

                          2,070   Gminy (county)

                         38,690   Solectwa (villages)

Religion: About 80-90% Catholic

	Poland	U.S.A.
Birth/Death Rate:		
Crude birth rate (per 1,000 population)	16	16
Crude death rate (per 1,000 population)	10	9
Natural increase Annual percent (Birthrate minus death rate)	0.6	0.7
Infant mortality rate (Annual number of deaths of infants under age 1 year per 1,000 births)	17.5	9.9
Life Expectancy at Birth (years)	71	75
Total Fertility Rate (average number of children a woman will have)	2.2	1.9
Percent of Married Women Using Contraception Total:	75	68
Modern Methods (Includes the pill, IUD, Sterilization, and other chemical and barrier methods)	26	63
Per Capita Gross National Product, 1987 (US$)	1,920.	18,430.

(GNP includes value of all domestic and foreign output)
(Population Reference Bureau 1989)

Language: Polish

Government: Socialist Constitution, 1944-1990

Economy: Urban industrialized country

                Industries includes: iron and steel,
                shipbuilding, textiles, mining of coal,
                copper, zinc, and lead. Agriculture
                includes: potatoes, sugar beets, rye,
                and rapeseed.

CHAPTER 2

TRADITIONS OF POLISH EDUCATION

Early History of Poland (Świecki 1977, 328-331; An Outline History of Polish Culture 1984, 15-24)

In the very early Middle Ages, from the fifth to the ninth centuries, several Slavonic tribes lived in the area of what is now Poland. The most powerful groups were the Wilanie, Vistulans, and the Polanie. The Polanie tribe gave Poland its name, since the word Polska originates with them.

Early rulers in Poland had a keen interest in education. For example, during the first half of the 11th century, King Boleslaus sent his son to Belgium to study. He returned with ideas from the field of architecture and monks from the Benedictine Order to serve as advisors to the king. Other intelligent kings who ruled during the 12th and 13th centuries felt good methods of agriculture should be taught to their people. Monks from France and Silesia came to Poland for this purpose.

As a result of contacts with other countries, Poland could participate in the culture of Southern and Western Europe. Christianity was introduced in 966 and soon the first cathedral and collegiate schools preparing priests opened.

During the 15th century, the Cracow Academy, established in 1364 by Casimir The Great, became one of Europe's distinguished universities. An atmosphere of tolerance and an open attitude towards new philosophical and scientific studies characterized the Academy. It became an international center for astronomical studies. Among its pupils was Nicolaus Copernicus.

Humanistic culture and religious tolerance developed early in the history of Poland. Many profes-

sors, who had suffered persecution in their home countries, sought refuge in Poland. As a result, dissident
schools began to appear where these professors and
young men who came from other countries could study.
Studies included the latest achievements in science,
especially in the natural sciences.

Several important Polish dissident schools were
set up. The Gymnasium of the Bohemian Brethren at
Leszno was an example of one important dissident
school.

Educational authors of the period perceived that
education had value in public life. Frycz Modrewski, a
social thinker of the Polish Renaissance, felt education was one of the foundations of effective government.   He insisted schools develop under state aus-
pices, schooling should be available for the peasantry,
and that teaching was the most honorable of all the
professions.

Educational thinkers of the Enlightenment drew
upon progressive ideas and in particular by Piarist
schools in reforming Poland's schools. A new era was
about to open in Polish education. Utilitarianism in
learning and a tendency to popularize knowledge came
into prominence in education.

Father Stanislaw Konarski founded the Colle-
gium Nobilium in 1740. The spirit of the Enlightenment
guided the teaching of philosophy, natural sciences,
geography, and history.

King Stanyslaus Augustus Poniatowski made an
important step toward the state taking over the entire
educational system. In 1765, he established the Gen-
try's Academy of the Cadet Corps, commonly called the
Knights' School. Graduates of this school were to make
reforms in ending ignorance, backwardness, and preju-
dice.

One of the greatest events in the history of
education in Poland took place in 1773. The Seym, the
national parliament, on the initiative of King Stanyslaus Augustus, established the Commission on National
Education, the world's first Ministry of Education.

The commission put education under state control
when a uniform system of national education came into
being.   Mathematics and the natural sciences received
considerable emphasis as did instruction in the Polish

language.   Other modern languages, ethics, and new
teaching methods were also an important part of the
uniform system.

Education at the elementary level received much
attention. The Commission tried to introduce technical
competence in agriculture, handicrafts, and trade into
the syllabus of the regular elementary school.

The production of textbooks was also given consideration by the Commission. New texts provided materials for the students' use. Old texts had provided
directions for the teacher.

Education During the Partitions of Poland (Świecki 1977, 329-331)

During these years, previous educational achievements were slowly and steadily reduced. In an attempt
to try to bring Poland to submission, the powers Russi-
fied and Germanized the schools. The use of the Polish
language was severely limited. The powers also at-
tempted to denationalize the country. Thus, the struggle to maintain Polish schools became one of national
survival.

The year 1773 was important to education as the
Commission for National Education was established.
This Commission was the first Ministry of Education in
the world. An important outcome of the Commission, was
the establishing of a uniform system of national education, from elementary to university level. Attempts
were made to integrate education with the life of the
country, its culture and history. They devoted much
attention to elementary education where attempts were
made to integrate elementary education with technical
competence in agriculture, handicrafts, and trade. The
Society for Elementary books aided the movement by the
preparation of textbooks which combined directions for
teachers with text materials for pupils. Challenges to
the work of the Commission occurred in both the Prussian and Austrian partition zones.

Let us now turn to an examination of education in
the three partitioned areas.

Russian Partition Sector

Polish schools were able to develop and flourish
in the Russian sector. Later educational reform in
Russia made use of the experiences of this Commission.

Further, many Polish educators (such as Adam Czarto-ryski, Ignacy Potocki and Hieronan Stroynowski) helped carry out this process.

Stroynowski, in particular, worked very hard to transform the school in Wilna into a university which occurred in 1802. Wilna became a center for sciences and the humanities as outstanding scientists and schol-ars came from both home and abroad.

The University of Wilna was important in other aspects. All high schools in Lithuania and Byelorrus-sia came under its control. In addition, they can maintain contacts with other Polish universities, notably the institutions in Warsaw. A strong cultural and scientific center developed in Wilna.

In the south-western part of the Ukraine, educa-tion was under control of Polish authorities. Local schools first trained all the children of noblemen or middle class while working class or country folk chil-dren did not receive an education. Tadeusz Czachi and Hugo Kołłątaj were able to set up their famous high school, in 1804, in Krzemieniec.

The Chamber of Education for School Affairs, run by Stanisław Potochn, restored and organized Polish high schools for craftsmen.

A prime concern of Potochn's was the spread of primary schools and their independence from parishes of the church.

These schools ran on voluntary fees and in spite of poor financial conditions in the country the number of schools increased by one-fourth (1/4th). In 1816 there were 120 primary schools; their number grew to 1,222 schools by 1821. The schools tried to reduce illiteracy. Vocational schools were set up for working people. In spite of these achievements, some of the nobility became discontent and reluctant to educate the peasant children. Eventually, Stanisław Grabowski became the new minister. He followed the will of the nobility in keeping peasants from education and as a result a complete decline of elementary schools oc-curred. By keeping peasants uneducated and unconscious socially, it was very difficult for them to become involved in the struggle for freedom. In small towns, on the other hand, schools developed and increased in

number, under the needs of industry. However, high fees
once again made it difficult for the poor to attend
school.

Prussian Partition Sector

In the Prussian sector the school reform favored
education not only for nobility, but also for country
youth. The schools were to be the main instrument of
Germanization.

The creation of the short-lived Duchy of Warsaw
(1807-12) made it possible to remove German influences
from the educational system in the central area of Poland. During this time the University of Warsaw,
founded by Alexander I, became more influential than
several other schools in the area. The future university included the five departments of medicine, law
theology, philosophy, and fine arts.

One of Poland's educators, Stanislaw Staszic, was
active during this period. He is remembered as the
founder of vocational training in Poland. Through his
work the Mining Academy in Kielce, the Forestry School
in Warsaw, and the Agronomic Institute in Marymount
were set up.

The Duchy of Poznań was another exception to the
German influence. There even existed Polish high
schools in the sector. In Silesia, Pomerania as well
as in Warmia, and Mazuria, local people resisted and
the Polish language was taught in the schools. In
addition, the clergy and teachers helped maintain the
language. Jósef Tompa became a symbolic figure in the
resistance as he edited papers and wrote handbooks in
Polish. One handbook, on the history of Silesia,
stressed the Polish character. Tompa's activity helped
lessen the German influence in Silesia.

Austrian Partition Sector

The least developed educational system occurred in
the Austrian sector. There were no elementary or high
schools. The University of Lwów was also at a very low
level. The language of instruction was first Latin,
then German. These problems and setbacks had a negative influence upon a level of societies education,
culture, and its ability to adjust to the changing
economic situation.

Polish schools were faced with the difficult task

of trying to teach their people knowledge of Poland's
past, and also how to keep pace with the fast developing European countries. Before partitioning, Poland's
financial situation was not strong. Poland had to rely
on private, most often lordly patronage, after the
partitioning. Several lordly families such as Czar-
toyski in Pułany, Stanisław Potocki, Józef Maksymil-
ian Ossoliński and others collected manuscripts,
monuments of art, and supported scientific research.
The most important Polish scientific institute was the
Friends of Learning Society founded in 1800 in Warsaw.
They assembled rich and influential amateurs and outstanding scientists and scholars.

The society received support first by the authorities of the Duchy of Warsaw and later by the Kingdom of
Poland. Activities included scientific research, research in history and language and natural history.

Thus, in spite of difficult conditions which
existed during and after the partition, the Polish
educational system made considerable progress. Many
people of intellect kept the educational lamp in Poland
burning.

Education After the Partitioning (Świecki 1977, 330-
331)

The building of a uniform educational system out
of the three separate systems under partitioning, was
not an easy matter.

Poland re-emerged as an independent state in
November 1918. An important task was to unify the
organization and standards of schools in the whole
country. Attempts were made to make up for the neglect
suffered during the partition period.

Many problems were present during this period.
Among the major problems were the development of
schools for national minorities and the training of
qualified personnel. In addition, school buildings
were lacking and all of these problems called for high
financial outlays.

In 1919, forty-seven percent of children who were
compelled to attend school actually did so. Many
teachers had only an elementary education and fewer
than one-third were graduates of teachers' colleges.
It was during this period that secondary education was

developed in Poland. During the 1920's, school attendance increased and the number of teachers and class
rooms grew.

Education in Poland during the 1930's came under
the influence of the economy. Unemployment and the
destitution of many people gave impetus to an outright
educational catastrophe. School attendance dropped
dramatically with estimates of over one million children without schooling.

Higher education developed in Poland during the
inter-war period. State universities were established
in Warsaw, Poznań, and Wilna. Various polytechnics,
academies, and trade schools developed. In 1919, the
National Library opened. Many scientific societies
and the future Polish Academy of Learning developed. In
the late 1930's, over thirty-two institutions of higher
learning existed. Higher education was exclusive.
Varying standards from elementary schools coupled with
high tuition fees helped give an elite character to the
universities.

In 1939, a new era of education in Poland was
about to happen.

Education In Poland During World War II
(Kolendo M., Zoziejow tajnego nauczania w latach oku-
pacji: 1941-44. Białystok, 1966).
(Miaso, Józef, Historia Wychowania, Panstwowe Wydaw-
nictwo Naukowe, Warszawa, 1980).
(The International Encyclopedia of Education, Volume 7,
Pergamon Press, Oxford, 1985. pp. 3951-3955).
(Poland A Handbook, Andrzej Świecki, Interpress Pub-
lishers, Warszawa, 1977).

On September 1, 1939, the Nazi forces of Adolph
Hitler invaded Poland and began a five year period of
extreme difficulty for the Polish educational system.
Through systematic reprisals, the Nazis sought to
annihilate the Polish culture. Nazi Governor - General, Hans Frank, wrote in his diaries:

... One should leave to the Poles only such educational opportunities as will show them the
hopelessness of their national situation... No
Pole shall rise above the rank of foreman ...
Every Pole must feel that we are not building for
him a state of law and order and that nothing for

him but one obligation: to work and to obey.
(Świecki 1977, 331)

Like many other public buildings, some school
buildings suffered destruction as a result of fighting
and some the Germans used for their offices and general
governmental buildings.

In addition to a lack of physical facilities,
there was a lack of trained teachers. Estimates are
that at least 16,000 teachers died in battle or as a
result of the extermination policy at concentration
camps.

During the occupation of Poland, Poles could not
attend secondary schools or institutions of higher
education as all of these schools remained closed.
Most primary schools remained open but under such
severe restrictions that they operated for only two
hours per day. No instruction in Polish history and
geography was allowed. Lower technical schools remained open, but their purpose became more craft-
oriented. However, the main reason the technical
schools were open was to provide the German industry
with skilled workers and forced labor.

An immediate backlash developed in response to the
closing of schools. Within a few weeks after occupa-
tion, students, parents, and teachers spontaneously
organized and secret teaching started to take place in
Poland. The leading role fell to the Polish Teachers'
Association and former pre-war school administrators. A
new, central leadership of the underground developed.
The newly developed organization was the OTN (Organi-
zacja Tajnego Nauczania) Teachers' Secret Organization.
The leadership consisted of five persons (Zygmunt
Norwicki, Czesław Wycech, Kazimierz Maj., Wacław
Tutoohiejski, and Teofil Wolenski) who were able to
unify the underground educational movement. The move-
ment was of wide range and covered the entire country.
Separate underground schools at the elementary, secondary, and higher education levels developed.

At about the same time, another underground center, the Committee of Public Education, developed under
the leadership of Kazimierz Pieracki.

In Autumn 1940, still a third organization sur-
faced as a branch of the Polish government in exile.
The Department of Education and Culture, developed
under the leadership of one of the OTN's leaders,

Czesław Wycech.   It contained three main sections:
Studies and Higher Education, Culture and Science, and
Training and Upbringing.

In German-occupied Poland teaching of forbidden
subjects either took place in classes or individual
lessons in the teachers' or pupils' private homes.
Teachers would add to the abridged Nazi curriculum
while teaching officially or unofficially during private or group meetings.   The range and effectiveness of
the secret teaching differed widely from province to
province.   Near the end of the war, the education of
every third or fourth pupil was made possible by including forbidden educational content.

Secret teaching in the Eastern territories and the
territories which had joined to Germany differed from
German occupied Poland.   Here individual or small group
instruction won as both teachers and pupils had to work
a compulsory 12 hour day.   Additionally, it was very
difficult to locate suitable classrooms.   Many Poles
had to vacate better flats which the Germans assumed
and had to live in overcrowded houses, so it was difficult to find teaching quarters.   The scope of education
in these areas was not nearly as wide as in Genevalna
Gubernia.   In 1943, 2600 teachers taught almost 50,000
students in elementary schools while in secondary
schools 680 teachers worked with 7500 pupils.

The situation in higher education was even worse:
officially, it ceased to exist in September 1939.
Poles could not enter higher schools, but in little
more than a year, the first underground studies started
at Warsaw University.   At the beginning only the humanistic departments started to work.   Over the years
other departments returned - mathematics, biology,
physical, chemical and biological sections, and geo-
graphical sections.   The two largest departments, law
and medicine, opened in 1944.   Medicine classes developed in local hospitals or clinics.   In all department of Warsaw University, about 3700 students under-
went higher education during this period.   Other higher
schools like Warsaw Polytechnic, The Trade School, The
Teachers' Institute and Theater Schools also organized
secret teaching.   This surreptitious educational process found favor in other towns, besides Warsaw.

The results of this immensely patriotic secret
teaching becomes clear when one considers that underground universities benefited some 10,000 students.   In
addition, 100,000 studied in underground secondary

schools and underground instruction in Polish language, history, and geography at elementary school level covered about one million children!

Underground education in Poland, ranks as a commendable achievement in the history of occupied Poland. As a result, hundreds of Polish children remained literate, patriotism cultivated and the will to fight did not go out. Therefore, when the war came to an end, authorities were able to move into a program of school reform.

Education in Poland After 1944

After World War II, many sweeping changes occurred in Poland. The Socialist Polish People's Republic came into being. Land reform and the nationalization of industry became a reality. Constitutional and political changes were essential features which drove the various educational reforms.

One of the first educational priorities was to reduce the large number of illiterates. Estimates ran as high as three million people, more than eighteen per cent of the population, who were illiterate. New programs were developed to help overcome this social condition.

A large amount of educational change was necessary at the elementary school level. The Socialist led educational leaders wanted to democratize schools, give an equal start to all children, and equalize urban and rural schools. Higher education also needed reconstruction and expansion after the ravages of World War II.

The newly nationalized industries needed trained workers and as a result vocational schools were developed.

Perennial problems such as lack of teachers, lack of facilities, and lack of supplies also plagued the new educational leaders. The large migration of people, caused by Poland's change in boundaries after World War II, also was a dilemma. As a result of rapid industrialization, people moved from the country to urban areas. The number of school age children rapidly increased after the war.

The 1952 Constitution addressed education in Article 61. "Citizens of the Polish People's Republic have the right to education."

CHAPTER 3

MANAGEMENT AND FINANCE

        Education in Poland has been a system of national
uniform education up to 1990 based upon the principles
of a socialist state and the constitution of 1952. The
primary goals include: citizens have a right to learn,
free education, and public and obligatory primary
schools. Other goals include a secondary educational
system and development of a university system. Additional goals are to improve qualifications of people in
industrial plants and work centers, and to provide a
state system of financial aid.

        The legal bases of the national educational system
in Poland are found in the Law on the development of
educational systems of 15.07.1961.

        The general provisions are:

    1.   The educational system prepares qualified
          employees for industry and culture.
    2.   Educational activities deliberately develop
          conscious and creative citizens for the
          Polish People's Republic.
    3.   Schools consider community life according
          to patriotism, freedom, peace, social justice
          and brotherhood with working classes of all
          countries.
    4.   Schools teach fondness and respect for work
          as well as respect for national values. They
          prepare students for active participation in
          the development, economy, and culture of Po-
          land.

        Education is a function of the State and schools
are secular in nature. Schools may open under coopera-
tives and religious institutions, but they are few.
(Several schools now operate under the Catholic
Church).

Poland's population is very homogeneous with few national minorities. However, where these minority populations exist, instruction occurs in the native language. (Examples are White Russians, Lithuanian, Ukrainian, Jewish, and Greeks). These schools are under State control and are declining in number.

Further, education at all levels is co-educational. In a few instances, either boys or girls receive instruction separately based upon the curriculum. Equity of sexes carries over into equity rights of children who come from different environments, social groups, or locations.

Central to education in Poland, is the deep social and economic reforms that are sweeping the country. Educational questions abound. How can education become modernized? How can newer teaching methods be used by teachers? How can instruction benefit from use of technology? How can the educational system become independent and self-governing?

Personnel at the Ministry of Education level ask these qeustions. There is a two-prong attack on these questions. First, few modernizing actions may occur due to the poor economy. Second, the Expert Committee for National Education report, nearing completion, will address these questions.

Management Structure

The control of the educational system in Poland occurs on two levels. One level is central agencies and the second level is local agencies. (Development of Education within 1986-1988, 1988, 14-20)

Central Agencies

The Minister of National Education (Chief organ of State Administration): Responsible for coordinating and supervising local agencies and other concerns at the national level. The Office of the Ministry of National Education is responsible for carrying out educational tasks.

Duties include:
1. determines syllabi which must be followed.
2. confirms school books and educational aids.
3. defines principles of operations in schools.

4.   determines conditions of admitting pupils to schools and pupils changing from one type of school to another type of school.
5.   forms networks of schools and other educational agencies.
6.   establishes standards for school supplies.
7.   develops principles of awarding scholarships.
8.   develops principles of meeting titles and diplomas.
9.   develops principles of examinations.

Local Agencies

Kuratorium-School Superintendent-On the State level, the school superintendent supervises schools and other educational agencies. In addition, Inspectors of Schools and head masters, are under the superintendent's control.

The Superintendent is to carry out State education laws and do orders, instructions, and directions from the Ministry of National Education.

Specific duties of the Superintendent include:
1.   determining personnel policies of the schools.
2.   selecting the staff.
3.   organizing teacher training and other self-improvement activities.
4.   visiting schools periodically to improve the level and effectiveness of the schools.

The superintendent also has control over other provincial institutions such as the educational information bureau and the pedagogical library. The educational emergency department (provide short-term care of children who are in danger - ie. families, drug, and alcohol abuse, etc.), and didactic and technical laboratories also come under the Superintendent's control.

The superintendents' council is advisory in nature and helps in making recommendations from time to time.

Other Types of Educational Administration at Communal Level

In districts where the population exceeds 50,000,

the Inspector of Schools manages educational affairs.
However, in towns where the population is under 50,000,
the chief officer of the town manages the education
affairs by the Inspector of Education.

The Inspector of Education is responsible for a
variety of activities carried out at the commune,
town, or district level. The primary duty is to supervise kindergartens, primary schools, and other educational agencies. Disputes of an educational nature
must be settled by the Inspector. These disputes occur
when State policies and social-economic needs of the
commune or town are in opposition. The Inspector also
is responsible for developing annual and long-range
reports highlighting the development of education,
schools, and educational agencies.

School

Each school is under the control of a Headmaster
and an Associate Headmaster(s) if school enrollment is
large. The Headmaster and the Pedagogical Council
cooperatively make educational decisions for the
school. The council includes: Headmaster, as Chair,
Associate Headmaster(s), teachers of the school, school
doctors, club-room educators, and representatives of
the parents. The Headmaster, in cooperation with the
Pedagogical Council, form the basis of educational
self-government.

Some duties of the Headmaster and the Pedagogical
Council are:
1.   planning and organizing educational work.
2.   implementing State educational guidelines.
3.   analyzing educational results.
4.   developing plans for additional education and
     professional self-development of teachers.
5.   developing cooperation with parents and
     local industries.
6.   confirming student grades and promotion.
7.   ratifying the annual educational plan of the
     school, school budget draft, and projection
     of expected expenses.
8.   providing opinions about employee awards and
     distinctions, pedagogical bonuses for teach-
     ers, awards, prizes, and distinctions for
     pupils.
9.   confirming student punishment, and giving
     opinions of candidates who are applying for
     advanced positions.

Finance

The Constitution of the Polish People's Republic guarantees free education. Funding for education comes from two main sources. One source is the State central budget and the second is revenue and expenditures of regional people's councils. Direct costs of education such as salaries, material costs, and capital costs come from these public monies.

Additional monies for education derive from funds of enterprises and welfare organizations, public funds for specific purposes, and personal earnings of people.

EDUCATIONAL EXPENSES

TABLE 3.1

STATE SPENDING FOR EDUCATION
(Statistical Yearbook 1988, 148)

Items	1980	1985 General	1986	1987	1985 Central Budget	1986	1987
	in millions of złotys						
TOTAL	61,094	331,596	395,957	497,194	14,470	17,870	24,626
Primary Schools	22,987	136,623	159,315	199,115	--	--	--
Primary Schools for Adults	64	217	--	--	--	--	--
General High School for Youths and Adults	2,943	12,958	15,419	19,748	117	186	290
Special General High School	969	5,676	6,515	8,135	--	--	--
Houses for children without parents (social service)	2,961	13,827	16,398	20,452	--	--	--
Dormitories and Scholarships for students of general education schools	544	2,247	2,794	3,537	9	7	9
Kindergarten in Cities	6,524	42,652	54,181	68,558	616	760	982
Clubs for children after school	--	8,537	10,123	12,269	2	3	2
Summer vacation and camps for children also winter break	1,066	4,830	5,809	6,830	91	105	149
Vocational Schools	8,626	37,932	44,029	58,724	2,712	3,304	4,252
Vocational Schools-governed by factories/industries	694	2,781	3,178	3,962	534	621	780
Dormitories and Scholarships for students in vocational schools	3,414	13,461	15,830	19,305	1,018	1,223	1,508
Education Improvements Centers	563	343	440	523	2	1	--
Additional Vocational School Units	--	--	--	6,694	--	--	393

TABLE 3.2

STATE EDUCATIONAL COSTS
(Development of Education Within 1986-88, 22)

	1985	1986	1987	1988 Plan
National income to be divided - in billions of złotys	8,527.3	10,579.1	13,285.0^X	13,660.0^{XX}
Education budget in general - in billions of złotys - and divided into:	497.5	603.4	745.0	867.6
1. current expenses of:	405.6	483.3	607.3	707.1
a) primary schools	152.5	178.5	226.5	261.5
b) elementary technical schools, secondary schools and post-grammar schools	96.5	116.0	145.0	167.5
c) colleges	74.0	87.5	110.1	132.0
d) agencies of care for children and youths	82.6	191.3	125.7	145.3
2. Capital expenditure and costs of general repairs:	91.9	120.1	137.7	160.5
a) primary, elementary, secondary and post-grammar schools and in agencies of care for children and youth	73.8	98.5	121.4^X	149.5
b) in colleges	18.1	21.5	26.3	41.0
Proportional share of education budget in a divided national income (2:3) - %	5.8	5.7	5.6	X

x) expected realization

xx) for 1987 prices

Source of information: data of the Ministry of National Education

TABLE 3.3

CURRENT SPENDING OF STATE BUDGET FOR SOCIAL
AND CULTURAL SERVICES
(Statistics Yearbook 1988, 100)

Items	1985	1986	1987	1985	1986	1987
	General			Central Budget		
	millions of złotys					
TOTAL	885771	1084241	1369170	269662	326761	417896
Education	331596	395957	497194	14470	17870	24626
General School System	262292	314652	—	9320	11740	—
Vocational Schools	69304	81305	—	5150	6130	—
Higher Schools	74001	87491	110061	73844	87419	109990
Culture and Art	59580	68546	89393	57128	62084	82771
Polish Radio and TV	3525	1754	1676	3525	1754	1676
Health Service and Social	402878	511205	647651	117925	153361	194170
Sport, Recreation, Tourism	17716	21042	24371	6295	6027	6339
Physical Culture and Sport	16205	20343	24148	5156	5948	6246

TABLE 3.4

CURRENT SPENDING ON HIGHER EDUCATION FROM
STATE BUDGET
(Statistical Yearbook 1988, 100)

Items	1980	1985	1986	1987	1985	1986	1987
	Total				Central Budget		
	millions of złotys						
TOTAL	18890	74001	87491	110061	73844	87419	109990
Science and Teaching of Didactics	14678	59828	71524	89047	59826	71521	89045
Financial and Social Aid for Students	2967	9374	9583	10056	9276	9622	10010
Reconstruction of Buildings and higher schools	—	4144	5444	8812	4144	5444	8812

1980	1981
83,200 million złotys (current prices)	104,100 million złotys (5.1% of total consumption of goods and services)
22,500 million złotys (current & capital expenditure on higher education)	25,000 million złotys (1.1% of the national expense

ANNUAL AVERAGE COST PER STUDENT IN

FULL—TIME HIGHER EDUCATION STUDIES

1966	1971	1981
26,700 złotys	56,800 złotys	76,600 złotys

Costs vary for different types of study. 1981 distribution:

Universities	70,100	Medical	100,200
Polytechnics	83,500	Marine	113,900
Engineering	81,200	Phys.Training	88,400
Agriculture	70,100	Art	97,000
Economic	48,500	Theological	45,700

CHAPTER 4

STRUCTURE OF THE EDUCATIONAL SYSTEM

The general structure of the educational system includes four major areas. They are: kindergartens for children age three to seven (0 level kindergarten compulsory); and eight-year standard primary schools for children age seven to fifteen (free and compulsory). Additionally there are: secondary schools for students age sixteen to twenty-one; and Universities, Polytechnics, Academies, and Colleges for students age nineteen and up.

A detailed analysis of each major area follows.

Kindergartens - Age 3-7

The general aims of education at this level center about the comprehensive development of children, their preparation for future learning, and their secure educational care while their parents are working.

Now there are two types of kindergarten schools in Poland. They are kindergarten schools and kindergarten sections. The kindergartens are open from ten to twelve months a year, with hours of operation fixed according to the needs and working hours of the parents. This feature is crucial as both parents usually must work outside the home. Hours of operation vary with most kindergartens in cities open from seven to eleven hours per day. Kindergartens in the villages open for five to eight hours per day. In rural areas, depending on the season of the year and the nature of the agricultural work, hours vary to meet these needs. Students assemble according to age with twenty-five to thirty students per group. Here they receive education, medical care, and food.

The kindergarten sections cluster in the primary schools where the child will attend in the future. They are open for eleven months a year and four to seven hours per day. Kindergartens may vary according

Figure 4.1

STRUCTURE OF POLISH EDUCATIONAL SYSTEM

GRADE   AGE

```
                                        ┌──────────────────┐
                                        │ Post-Graduate    │
                                        └──────────────────┘
                    ┌──────────────────────────────────┐
                    │   Universities                    │
                    │   Polytechnics                    │     19-up
                    │   Academies                       │
                    │   College                         │
                    └──────────────────────────────────┘

  5    ┌──────────┐        ┌──────────────┐      ┌──────────────┐
  4    │  Lycea   │        │ Secondary    │      │ Shortened    │
  3    │          │        │ Technical    │      │ Vocational   │   16-21
  2    └──────────┘        │ Schools      │      │ Schools      │
  1                        │    &         │      └──────────────┘
                           │ Vocational   │
                           │ Lyea         │
                           └──────────────┘

  8    ┌──────────────────────┐
  7    │                      │
  6    │                      │
  5    │                      │
  4    │  Primary             │                                  7-15
  3    │  Schools             │
  2    │                      │
  1    │                      │
       └──────────────────────┘

                                                                   6
  0    ┌──────────────────────┐
       │ ─ ─ ─ ─ ─ ─ ─ ─ ─ ─  │                                  3-5
       │  Kindergartens       │
       └──────────────────────┘
```

to local needs, number of children and the public needs. Children age six assemble in zero class with seven to twenty-five children in each section. This zero class is compulsory.

School #77, Bialystok, Poland, is a typical exam ple of education at this level. Children, age three to seven years, come from Bialystok and nearby areas. Here two hundred students are broken into seven groups of thirty students each. Each group has two teachers, with one working for five hours in the morning and the other for five hours in the afternoon. It is possible for children to attend this school from 6:00 a.m. until 5:00 p.m. There are no set hours for attendance. However, the child may not stay longer than the working hours of the parents plus commuting time. Breakfast starts at 8:30 a.m., lunch at noon and afternoon tea at 2:30 p.m.

Teachers at this school have graduated from the University, Teachers College, or Teachers Grammar School. People with no prior professional preparation for teaching may qualify by attending the extra-mural studies program of the University. The Director of the kindergarten received her appointment from the Kurator (school superintendent) who may also remove the Direc- tor if necessary. Teachers at this school had no voice in the selection. She received appointment on the basis of her educational level, prior practice with children of this level, and because of her flexibility.

The school program has four areas. First, health-physical activities, gymnastics, and sports. Second, social-behavior and group social interactions. Third, aesthetics-music, drawing, and construction, and fourth, mind-mental development with an emphasis on mathematics. Time for lessons vary with twenty minute lessons for the younger children and twenty-five to fifty minutes for the older children.

The six year-old students (0 class) have construc- tion activities of simple rules from physics and other sciences. Pre-reading, in which the child masters twenty-two letters and numbers from one-ten, addition and subtraction and sets. School priorities are constantly shifting from stressing academic and then to social and then stressing more social than academic priorities. The teachers report they teach academics using simulation games.

Parents of the children are very helpful. Since

the school has a small budget, the parents literally helped construct and provide materials for the building. Parents attend meetings three times per school year.

The parents pay for each child per month based upon their income. The remainder of the fees come from the government. During the 1988-89 school year, the fee was 7,500 złotys per child, per month. This would represent about twenty percent of the income of one parent.

Evaluations of the children are on an individual basis, with the parents coming to school for conferences. In addition, teachers of the six-year olds send a report to the teacher in the primary class.

In academic year 1988-89, one hundred eighty children could not attend this school due to a lack of space and teachers. Handicapped, children of teachers, single parents, and large families (four or more children) were selected. Further, the parent is free to take the child elsewhere to another school.

Special education classes for students who may not be able to function in a regular class or due to handicaps or diseases attend a special school. Here one teacher and two aides work with ten children. Parents give permission for their child to enter the program and then attend a special school. The school and the teachers would prefer to mainstream these children. They are unable to do so now because of lack of funds and lack of physical facilities, two major problems which face all levels of education in Poland.

School #77 in Białystok meets the educational needs of children. However, in the rural areas of Białystok Wojewodztwo (state) differences soon emerge. These schools lack qualifications. Therefore, graduates of grammar school branches are only able to provide education for the six year olds (zero class). Often no meals or perhaps one meal is offered. The State government maintains that schools are equal across all of Poland, but visible differences soon become clear as one sees schools in urban and in rural areas. As a result, very different future educational paths are available to students from urban and rural areas.

TABLE 4:1

Syllabus - Primary Schools (Development of Education Within 1986-1988, 38-39)

Subjects	Standard (Grade)								Teacher's hours
	1st	2nd	3rd	4th	5th	6th	7th	8th	
1. Polish	8	8	8	7	6	5	5	5	52
2. Russian	-	-	-	-	3	3	2	2	10
3. History	-	-	-	1	2	2	2	2	9
4. Theory of Community	-	-	-	-	-	-	1	2	3
5. Social and natural environment	1	2^X	2^X	-	-	-	-	-	5^X
6. Biology and hygiene	-	-	-	2	2	2	2	1	9
7. Geography	-	-	-	2	2	2	1	1	8
8. Physics	-	-	-	-	-	2	2	2	6
9. Mathematics	5^X	5^X	5^X	5	5	5	4	4	38^X
10. Chemistry	-	-	-	-	-	-	2	2	4
11. Work-technology	2^X	2^X	2^X	2	2	2	2	2	16^X
12. Fine Arts	2^X	2^X	2^X	1	1	1	1	1	11^X
13. Music	2^X	2^X	2^X	1	1	1	1	1	11^X
14. Physical Education	2^X	3^X	3^X	2	2	2	2	2	18^X
15. Defensive Training	-	-	-	-	-	-	-	0.5^{XX}	0.5
16. Pupil's Practices	-	-	-	-	-	1	1	1	3
17. An hour for the form master	-	-	-	1	1	1	1	1	5
18. Obligatory pupils' hours	$(22)^-$	$(24)^-$	$(24)^-$						
	20	20	21	24	27	29	29	29.5	199.5
19. Obligatory for some groups of pupils. correcting gymnastics	2	2	2	-	-	-	-	-	6
20. Didactic and compensating classes	2	2	2	2	1	1	1	1	12
21. Optionally: West European language (at choice)	-	-	-	-	-	-	2	2	4
22. Physical games	2	2	2	-	-	-	-	-	6
23. Recreation and sports classes	-	-	-	2	2	2	2	2	10
24. Circles of interests			2						X
25. School choir			2						X
26. School orchestra			2						X
Obligatory for all pupils (per year.) Reading information training	1	1	2	2	3	3	4	4	20

^{X} - Reduction of the week total amount of hours in the 1st standard - from 22 to 20, in the 2nd standard - from 24 to 20, in the 3rd standard - from 24 to 21.

Polish may not be reduced in number of hours. Subjects included in the syllabus may not be eliminated. In addition, particular subjects may not be reduced by more than one hour a week. The benefit of the child, the working conditions at school, available personnel and equipment all should be taken into consideration when making reductions.

xx - Classes in defensive training in the 8th standard occur every two weeks, one hour each or during one semester for one hour a week.

Notes: Under each standard, 1st standard = 1st grade, number of hours per week to that subject.

Items 1-18 are the total requirements.

Item 18 is a summary of total hours per week for each class. Example: 6th grade = 29 hours. Teacher's hours appear in column and total hours in column 18.

Items 19-26, availability depending upon each school, teachers available, etc.

Item 20, Didactic and Compensating Classes - refers to extra help given students - as an example, a Social Worker.

Item 23, refers to after school activities.

Item 24 - Circles of Interests - usually refer to a related or subject area. Example - Physics, Olympics.

Item 17 - An hour for the form master - each class has a master teacher who acts like a homeroom teacher for the whole class. Discusses class conduct, how to achieve better grades and general counseling.

Item 11 - Work-Technology -in grades 1-2-3 all boys and girls do common items together. At Grade 4, a deviation occurs. Boys - shop work - hammers, drills: Girls - sewing, kitchens, and food preparation. Work-technology occurs in special rooms. The boys are in one room and the girls are in another room with a separate curriculum for each. Old male and female roles continue in Poland and in most of Central Europe.

X's - Line 18 - Means Headmaster can reduce in these areas from the required number of hours. Example: Class 1 - total hours should be 22, but can be cut back

to 20.   In Class 1 - Math, Work-technology, fine arts,
music, physical education classes may be cut.   Polish,
Social and Natural Environment may not be receive a
reduction.

Primary Schools - Age 7-15

The most basic part of the Polish school system is
the eight standard, obligatory, free, uniform primary
school. Graduates have the option to compete for
admission to the secondary system of technical and
grammar education; however, a qualification entrance
examination is necessary. A child must start primary
school during the year in which he or she turns seven.
The child then remains, until completing eight years or
until turning seventeen.

The comprehensive progress of all pupils in their
social, mental, moral, and physical aspects are factors
in the curriculum. Pupils prepare for learning at
secondary technical and grammar schools as well as the
world of work.

Special students (defined as those with psycho-
physical deviations possible to end at school) may take
supplementary individual classes.   On the other hand,
talented students can attend schools of sports, fine
arts, ballet, music, and choir, orchestra.

While primary schools across Poland vary, School
#307 in Warsaw (im. Króla Jana III Sobieskiego), is
representative.

School is in session five days per week.   In
previous years students attended one additional Saturday per month. Schools across Poland have gone to the
five day schedule.

The eight-year old 1-8 school was comprised of the
following classes:

	Level	Number of Classes per Level	Number of Students per Class
One teacher per	1	4	5
class who stays	2	4	35
with same students	3	4	35
in all subjects.			

Each subject taught	4	Breaks of	3	40
by special subject	5	5-10-15 min.	3	40
matter teacher.		between classes.		
Teacher will	6		5	30
stay in lab, other-	7		7	30
wise teachers	8		7	30
change rooms.				

This particular school has two sessions or changes per day. The 1st change is from 7:45 a.m. to 11:00 a.m. for younger children and to 1:00 p.m. for older students. The second change for younger students starts at 11:00 a.m. or noon until 3:00 p.m. and 1:00-5:00 p.m. for older students. Due to a lack of adequate school facilities in Poland, flexible schedules of one, two, or even three changes are normal. Changes in a school day are particularly bothersome for many Polish parents. (See Chapter 6 - Parental Views of Education)

Teachers' time schedules also vary from three to eight hours per day with every teacher teaching eighteen hours weekly.

The school's administrative structure is comprised of one Headmaster, two Associate Headmasters, and one School Pedagogy (Social Worker). The social worker's duties include helping disadvantaged students and their parents. Additional duties include providing consultation to teachers concerning social and academic problems of the school's students.

School opened this morning for students in all classes in grades six, seven, and eight, their teachers, and an Associate Headmaster in a large meeting. Topics discussed included: how to save and re-cycle paper, future school excursions, and introduction of new members who were coming onto the school council. Additional topics were a projected exchange trip for students to a school in Vienna, Austria, and vandalism in the school. Vandalism and a general lack of respect for buildings and equipment seems widespread in Poland.

Class 3, Social and Natural Environment, one teacher and thirty-seven students are attending to a typical day's schedule. First, the teacher examines homework from the previous lesson, then presents new material, answers questions, and finally assigns new homework.

Class 5, Geography, was of special interest due to new equipment. The thirty five students in this room had small 9" individual student globes, three large 14" globes, and two slated globes. In addition, many new maps were available for study. Before the teacher and students had only very old German maps available for classroom use. Now a special company can supply such teacher materials.

The teacher in Class 7, Physics, had an equipment room containing purchased and student made equipment. She was extremely proud of the talented students who return after a regular class day to work on special physics projects. The students participate in a Physics Olympics program. As a result many of her students do not take the Physics Grammar School Entrance Exam - the students do well in her Physics class!

The school is responsible for Swietlica (Homework Rooms) for students in grades one, two and three whose parents are working. Special teachers come into the school to operate this program until 5 p.m. The program includes resting, doing homework and waiting for parents.

Older students in grades four to eight simply become latch key children. They are loose to fend for themselves until parents return home.

Students may bring lunches from home (called a second breakfast in Poland--sandwiches, etc.) or buy a dinner in the school lunchroom. Students pay by the month for a dinner (dinner in Poland is a heavy meal served about 3 p.m. in homes and restaurants). Teachers in grades one, two and three supervise a special break time for student lunches. Students in grades four to eight are not under a classroom teacher's guidance.

Secondary Schools - Ages 15-16-19 (Graduation Examinations)

Secondary schools include four-year Lycea which prepare students for college and university studies. Four-year technical schools and vocational Lycea prepare students for becoming qualified workers with a secondary education. Three-year (essential) schools prepare students to become qualified workers (vocations such as hairdresser and agriculture). Students who graduate from both the Lycea and the Secondary Technical school have no profession and they must continue further education. Students who graduate from the Essential Schools have a profession.

Students gain admission to the various secondary schools on the basis of entrance examination results and achievement at primary school. Admission standards also consider results from subject matter competitive examinations in Humanities, Science, and Mathematics, and other special achievements of the student. Special achievement means good students with scores of 5's and 4's attend a grammar school while students whose grades are not as high attend the Secondary Technical track. If the grades are still lower, these students enter into the Essential Schools track.

About ninety-seven percent of primary school graduates continue and learn at the various secondary schools. These schools are also free of charge.

Lycea Schools

Poland's academic students choose the four-year Lycea. The student graduates after completing the top form-4th (4th class), must pass a school leaving exam, and receives a certificate of secondary education. The student then has the right to take the entrance examination into University, college, polytechnics, or academies.

Students may select one of the following tracks, 1.) Mathematics and Physics (Polish people believe this is the elite track), 2.) Biology and Chemistry, 3.) Humanistic, 4.) Standard (General or Basic), 5.) Sports, and 6.) Classic (very few schools). Students may also choose pedagogical track, on an experimental basis only, in a few schools.

A school year contains two semesters and one form (class) lasts for one school year which is about ten months.

TABLE 4.2
Syllabus - Grammar School (Development of Education Within 1986-1988, 1988, 40-41)

NUMBER OF HOURS PER WEEK
FORM (GRADE)

Subjects	1st	2nd	3rd	4th	Total
1. Polish	4	4	4	4	16

NUMBER OF HOURS PER WEEK
FORM (GRADE)

Subject	1st	2nd	3rd	4th	Total
2. Russian	2	2	2	2	8
3. West-European Language	3	3	3	3	12
4. History	2	2	2	2	8
5. Theory of Community	-	-	1	2	3
6. Theory of Religions	-	-	1	-	-
7. Biology with hygiene and environment protection	2	2	2	2	8
8. Geography	1	1	2	1	5
9. Mathematics	4	4	3	4	15
10. Physics with astronomy	3	3	2	2	10
11. Chemistry	2	2	2	-	6
12. Fine Arts	1	1	-	-	2
13. Music	1	1	-	-	2
14. Work-technology	2	2	2	2	8
15. Physical Education	2	2	2	2	8
16. Defensive Training	1	1	2	-	4
17. Facultative classes[1]	-	-	-	2	2
18. Preparation for family life	0.5	0.5	0.5	0.5	2
TOTALS	31	31	29	27	118

Extra Classes
A. Obligatory

	1st	2nd	3rd	4th	Total
1. Reading and information, training	3 hours a year each form				
2. Supplementary subjects [2]	-	2	2	2	6
3. Pupil's practices during a school year	70 hours each in the 1st form				X
TOTALS	31	33	31	29	124

B. Optional

	1st	2nd	3rd	4th	Total
1. Latin	2	2	2	2	8
2. Sports and recreation classes	2	2	2	2	8
3. Circle of interests	as the need, and possibility				
4. Artistic classes (choir, orchestra)	arise - 1-2 hours a week for				
5. School theatre, dancing group, etc.	for a class				

1.   Facultative classes are according to the type: humanistic, mathematical and physical, natural, technical. Classes organized in intersection groups. Pupil chooses one type of class.

2.   **Supplementary Teaching Subjects:** propaedeutics of economic sciences, theory of law,

propaedeutics of philosophy, problems of
contemporary civilization, scientific information with science, elements of computer
science, environment protection and forming,
selected problems of pedgogics and psychology. Classes are taught in groups up to thirty
pupils for two hours a week in a year course
or for one hour a week in a two-year course.
Pupils choose one subject for one or two
years.

Graduates of the Lycea do not have a profession
upon completion of this level and so must continue in
higher levels of education.

Secondary Technical Schools

Students with grades from the primary school (3's
to 4's) choose the Secondary Technical track. These
schools prepare qualified workers and students who
graduate from these schools do have a profession and
certificate. There exists a variety of four, five, and
six year programs that students may choose. However,
most technical programs are five years in length.
Examples include: Economic schools, art schools, music
schools, theater production and staging schools. Other
examples include nursing schools, teacher training
schools for kindergarten and elementary grades one, two
and three, and schools connected with factories.
Secondary Technical Schools are broken into two groups,
technical schools and vocational Lycea schools.

Several additional examples may be of help.
Nurses may take a four or five year program. A few
schools in Poland still offer a four year program.
This course prepares nurses to work with very young
children who are still in cribs. The five year program
is broken into the regular four year program with the
certificate of secondary school education. The fifth
year is a practical training course for the vocational
diploma. They qualify as nurses.

An example of a six year program is the one which
prepares candidates to become teachers of kindergarten
and grades one, two, and three in the primary school.
After completing an entrance examination, the candidate
takes a practical artistic talent test. The test
establishes if the person has abilities in these areas.
Then the student completes the regular four year lycea
school. The student passes the exam for the certificate of secondary education, and continues into the

last two years of the program. Here the actual pedagogical classes   prepare teachers for kindergarten,
elementary grades one, two and three and music education.

     The Vocational Lycea differs widely from the
Technical Schools. The Vocational Lycea schools are of
a four year duration; students complete the certificate
of secondary education, but do not have advanced titles
or certification. They qualify to enter the work
force. The possession of a proper title or certification is of crucial importance in Poland for it usually
carries with it additional salary. This type of school
developed during the 1980's. Today the number of these
schools is declining due to extreme problems of students with poor training and low motivation. One of
the recommendations from the Committee for National
Education is the cancellation of the Vocational Lycea
type schools. See Chapter 8 for additional information
on the Committee.

     On the other hand, Secondary Technical Schools are
usually of a five year duration. Students complete the
certificate of secondary education and earn a vocational title of Technician in a specific job. This distinction, once again, means more money.

     Technical High School in Białystok, Poland, has
been in existence for over forty years.   It is one of
about 100-150 technical high schools in Poland.   Three
areas of the curriculum offered to students are, 1.)
General Building, 2.) Surveying, and 3.) Roads and
Bridge Building. The staff of fifty-five are individuals who have architecture or Engineering backgrounds.
General teachers such as Polish and foreign language,
and those with practical job experience may join the
staff.   The staff members have all graduated from
Universities, Polytechnical Schools, or who have practical job experience and have also taken general
courses in pedagogy.

     Dormitories are available for students attending
Technical High School, as this is the only school of
this type in the whole Białystok Wojewodztwo (State).
Therefore, many students live in the dormitories. The
government provides a partial grant to pay for the
facilities, but parents must also bear some of the
costs.

     Students who complete primary school (elementary
school) usually choose the five-year technical school

or the three-year technical school and complete an exam. Some students choose a two-year job school without an exam and go into work force. Students after completing six years in primary, leave to attend this two-year job school. Students do not receive the total curriculum of grades seven and eight but it prepares students for work. The job school does not provide qualifications or certification and the student enters the work force. There is competition for spaces in the program and more candidates apply than there are spaces available.

In 1988-89 the figures were:

Program	Available Spaces	Number of Candidates
General Building	90	180
Surveying	50-60	Fewer than spaces
Roads and Bridges Building	30	30

Entering students take the entrance examination of the Polish language and mathematics. Sometimes the candidates must submit drawings. Failing students have two options, 1.) Attend the two-year job school, or 2.) repeat the exam.

Figures on graduates show most students stay and work in the Białystok area. Many men go into the military for a two year period, and about fifteen percent go on to higher education (Example: Polytechnics).

An interesting feature of the school is that each year during May, all students do a one-month on-the-job training program. Students, in groups of ten to fifteen, go out into the community to work with teachers and on-site personnel supervising the work experience.

The students must complete oral and written examinations. The written portion is over the general subjects. A committee of three teachers conducts the oral exam portion. Pass rate is 95% with 5% failure.

The school lacked physical space. Thirty classes had to be scheduled into twenty-one classrooms. So, once again, two and sometimes three changes were necessary to complete the schedule. Classes meet for a forty five minute period with ten minute and twenty minute breaks scheduled.

A female engineer, who lectured and used the overhead projector, taught a class in the Bridges program. Twenty-four 2nd form students were present with eight female and sixteen males. Her lecture was about designing general structures of buildings and mechanics of building in particular. The teacher first presented the theory portion (type of roof), and made a sketch. Students who had been working in groups, came to the chalkboard and did the theoretical background portion of the lesson.

This teacher later admitted she had to teach material exactly as it was in the program (standard syllabus), even though newer theories were available to the profession.

The teaching load per week is eighteen hours. These dedicated teachers do their jobs as they could earn more money in jobs outside of school.

Shortened Vocational Schools

Students who enter these three year, shortened, vocational schools receive preparation within various vocations or jobs. However, the students receive a lower standard of preparation. Class requirements are toward practical application of the subject (example: hairdresser, auto mechanic). These students do not take an examination for graduation and they will not have completed the certificate of secondary education but they do have a profession. These students do have the option of later attending a secondary technical school. Here it is possible to earn a certificate of secondary education and pursue higher education. Therefore, it is possible for students to pursue forms of higher education.

When examining the chart of the structure of Polish Educational System, there is no connecting line from the various primary schools to the Shortened Vocational Schools, no entrance examination. By law, there is no official entrance examination into these schools. In fact some of the shortened vocational programs are more popular and so they often organize unofficial tests. They may be of a general nature and often are oral.

Students may eventually take the entrance examination and gain admission to a three year Secondary Technical School designed to serve graduates of the Shortened Vocational Schools. Upon completion, they may sit for the certificate of secondary education and continue to higher education.

Special Schools

There are special schools at the secondary level, but attending students do not receive a certificate of secondary education (Certificate of Maturity). In addition, a few special vocational schools exist train blind students for professions such as massage work. Special students can attend regular secondary schools, but choose the grammar schools. These special students could go on to higher education, but usually choose not to. There seem to be a few schools for hearing impaired and blind students. For a further examination of the preparation of special education teachers refer to Chapter 5.

Universities, Polytechnics, Academies, and Colleges

Students' entering these higher forms of Education in Poland must complete the certificate of secondary education (certificate of maturity) and pass an entrance examination. The major purposes of education at these levels are to complete the required studies, secure the university degree, and conduct scientific research. Course work may vary from four to six years of study. Studies culminate by writing and defending a Master's thesis with a Master's degree confirmed. However, some Polytechnics and some colleges, or in some courses, a certificate of Engineering is possible without the M.A. degree. These students have a higher vocational preparation, but without the scientific portion.

Universities

Universities are humanistic oriented and concern themselves with basic and applied research. Therefore, departments teach academic subjects. Example: Mathematics. The subject stands on its own merit, but there is no interest in applying the subject.

There are twelve universities in Poland:
Jagiellonian University - 1364
Wrocław University - Founded 1702, Rebuilt 1945
University of Warsaw - 1818
Catholic Lublin University (KUL) - 1918

University of Adam Mickiewicz at Poznań (U.AM) -1919
University of Maria Curie - Skłodowska in Lublin (UMCS) - 1944
Łódź University - 1945
University of Mikolaj Kopernik in Toruń (UMK) - 1945
Silesian University - 1968
University of Gdańsk - 1970
University of Szczecin - 1979

Polytechnics

Polytechnics concern themselves with knowledge and its application within specialized fields of study. Examples of Polytechnics would include Engineering, Construction, Computer Science, Electronics, Building, and Civil Engineering.

Academies

Academies are schools designed to teach special advanced instruction in areas such as Medicine (six year program), Fine Arts, Economics, Agriculture, Sports, and Military.

Colleges

Colleges are schools offering specialized instruction. One example would be teacher training. Teachers prepare to teach the higher levels of primary and secondary education. The four year program prepares future teachers in academic disciplines (Mathematics, Science, for example) and in Pedagogy, and Psychology.

Postgraduate Studies

Postgraduate studies in Poland centers around Ph.D. work and continuing studies. However, some programs have had to cancel their Doctoral studies programs due to students not being successful in completion of the programs. Several factors enter here. First, there are very few candidates in some programs. Second, there is no pressure from their work place for advanced study. Third, there is a lack of interest and motivation on the part of the candidates. Fourth, there is a lack of support (secretarial, computer, research materials, basic communication tools) for the candidate. All work is done by the candidate on their own. Fifth, often it is not an economic advantage to pursue postgraduate studies. It is simply not worth the effort and so many candidates drop out along the way.

Certain disciplines have set up special postgraduate studies centers for continuing education. The most notable example in Poland is in the area of medicine.

Students in Poland usually travel the following academic path:

* A student enters the University. Next the student pursues a five year program culminating in the M.A. degree.

* The person secures employment, but continues to work on and completes post-graduate studies. Upon completing the Ph.D. degree, the person is given the rank of adiunkt (senior assistant lecturer), and title dr.

* An eight year period occurs between the Ph.D. and the next highest rank dr. hab. (Doctor Habilitowany). Evaluations are given every three years on work to date with a decision to keep or fire the person.

* Person must write a scholarly work (book) and be approved by a board of peers. The candidates must then gain approval by the C.K.K. (Central Qualifications Commission) at national level. Title used is dr. hab. and has rank of docent.

* There are two levels among the class Professor, one a lower level and one a higher level. There seems to be a rather artificial distinction between classes, but the major difference relates to salary. In the workload, production of professional books and articles, advising of Ph.D., MA, and other students, the ranks seem to be about the same. Productivity is an individual's own work and progress in a specific area or niche of academic work.

How does an individual achieve this status? Some general conditions include having a cadre of students, and working on a special theory or interest within a discipline. Also being the author of published articles and books based upon the research interest area and serving as a tutor for M.A. and Ph.D. students is necessary.

Certain disciplines or departments only have these Professor classes. There is a quota of so many faculty members at certain ranks in each department. The Minister of Education now determines the quotas. Therefore, some departments can nominate professor candidates to the CKK (Central Qualifications Commission) at the national level.

At this point, a further word in explanation of the dependency relationship formed as one moves from M.A. to ordinary professorship is helpful. In Poland, it is quite usual and normal for a student to start at the university level with a top, ordinary professor and complete the M.A. At this point, often the professor will ask a student to join his or her cadre of students and continue to pursue the Ph.D. The dr. hab. degree, then the extra ordinary professorship, and finally as ordinary professorship are possible. Now the newly created ordinary professor has developed a cadre of people and the process continues.

There are certain advantages such as a support system while going through the steps, but disadvantages also occur. The ordinary professor is in charge and requires people below to do all forms of work.

CHAPTER 5

TEACHERS AND TEACHER TRAINING

Teacher qualifications are an important educational issue in Poland. Current estimates are that over
forty thousand non-qualified teach each year in Poland.
Further, numerous University graduates will not enter
the teaching profession due to the low salaries.

Teachers in Poland attain qualification through
several training programs. The following chart contains necessary levels of training to teach at the
different schools.

Teacher Level   Qualifications
KINDERGARTEN   *Initial Teaching Studies
                               two year program
                                      OR
                             *University or College
                               graduates
                             five-year program with
                                  M.A. degree
                                      OR
                             *Extramural Studies at a
                             University - three-year
                                  program

PRIMARY
  Grades One-Two-Three   *Same as kindergarten
                             teachers as above

  Grades Four through   *University or College
  eight   graduate
                             five-year program with
                             M.A.

LYCEA   *Same as primary teacher
                             in grades four through
                             eight as above.

SECONDARY TECHNICAL
   Academic subjects   *University or College
                                        graduate. Five-year
                                        program with M.A.
                                        degree.

   Vocational subjects   *Depends on subject.
                                        Teachers who do not have
                                        the M.A. degree.
                                        Teachers with no or some
                                        degree of higher level
                                        training.
                                        Teachers with Master's
                                        degrees in Engineering.

Teacher Training Programs

Initial Teaching Studies - This program prepares teachers for service as a kindergarten or primary teacher of grades one through three. Graduates from the Lycea attend post-grammar school courses for a two-year period.

The following chart is a syllabus of required subjects, with the number of hours per week per subject. Also provided are the total number of hours during the study per subject, and scheduled examinations.

Syllabus of Required Subjects

| Subjects | Number of hours a week | | | | Number of Hours during studies | | Exam during semester | |
| | 1st year | | 2nd year | | 1st year | 2nd year | semester Totals | |
	1st Semester 20 wks	2nd Semester 17 wks	1st Semester 19 wks	2nd Semester 10 wks				
Selected problems of philosophy and sociology	2	2	-	-	74	-	74	II
Pedagogics	2	3	-	-	91	-	91	II
General psychology	2	1	-	-	57	-	57	II
Progress - educational psychology	-	-	3	2	-	74	74	IV
Biomedical basis of progress and education	2	2	-	-	74	-	74	II

Subjects	Number of hours a week				Number of Hours during studies		Totals	Exam during semester
	1st year		2nd year		1st year	2nd year		
	1st Semester 20 wks	2nd Semester 17 wks	1st Semester 19 wks	2nd Semester 10wks				
Technical means of (initial) teaching	-	-	2	1	-	46	46	-
Methodology of initial teaching with practice	-	2	2	2	34	56	90	-
Methodology of initial teaching and educational work with practice	4	4	4	5	148	122	270	II
Principles of science on Polish language	3	2	2	1	94	46	140	III
Children's literature with culture of spoken language	-	-	1	2	-	56	56	IV
Loghopaedics (Techniques to reduce speech problems)	-	-	-	2	-	20	20	-
Principles of initial teaching of mathematics	2	2	2	1	74	46	120	III
Principles of social-natural environment science	1	1	2	2	37	56	93	IV
Music with methodology	2	2	2	2	74	56	130	-
Fine arts with methodology	2	2	2	2	74	56	130	-
Physical education with methodology	1	2	2	2	54	56	110	-
Work-technology with methodology	2	1	2	3	57	66	123	-
Playing an instrument	2	2	2	2	74	56	130	-
Defensive Training	2	1	-	-	57	-	57	-
Course in a foreign language	2	2	2	2	74	56	130	-
TOTAL HOURS	31	31	31	31	1147	368	2015	II
Optional classes: 1. Sports training	2	2	2	2	74	56	130	
2. Creative activities	-	-	-	2	-	20	20	

Subjects	Number of hours a week				Number of Hours during studies		Exam during
	1st year		2nd year				semester
	1st Semester 20 wks	2nd Semester 17 wks	1st Semester 19 wks	2nd Semester 10 wks	1st year	2nd year	Totals
3. Methodology of education in the Polish Scouts' Association	-	2	-	-	34	-	34
4. School choir	2	2	2	2	74	56	130
5. Course in the second foreign language	2	2	2	2	74	56	130

Upon completion of the program, students qualify as teachers for kindergarten and primary school grades one through three, but have not earned the M.A. degree. (Ministry of National Education of the Polish People's Republic, 1988, 60-61)

Extramural Studies - This program also prepares candidates for teaching at the kindergarten and primary school grades one through three level. Upon completing the Initial Teaching Studies Program, successful candidates may take an entrance examination and enter the three-year Extramural Studies program at a university.

The six semester program follows:

Syllabus of Extramural Studies

Subject	Hours of classes		Total	Exams	Papers
	Lectures	Activating Classes			
History	20	20	40	1	
Theory of political sciences with political economy	10	10	40	1	
Logics	10	10	20	1	
Foreign Language	-	-	-	1	
Psychology: of personality clinical, social and educational	20	70	90	2	X
Pedagogics: history of education, didactics, theory of education, social pedagogics, special pedagogics	70	90	160	3	X

Syllabus of Extramural Studies

Subject	Hours of classes Lectures	Activating Classes	Total	Exams	Papers
Theory and practice of initial teaching	20	40	60	1	X
Educational system on a comparative background	5	10	15		
Management of the educational system and school law	5	10	15		
Methods of pedagogical research and statistics	10	30	40		
Loghopaedics	-	20	20		
Re-education	-	20	20		
Facultative classes	-	80	80		X
Pedagogical practices	-	5	5		
Monographic lecture	20	-	20		
Graduate's seminar	100	100	100	1	
TOTAL	190	515	705	11	

(Ministry of National Education of the Polish People's Republic, 1988, 58-59)

COMMENTS:
    Activating classes - seminars, discussion groups or conversation.

    Loghopaedics - techniques to reduce speech problems.

    Re-education - Techniques to reduce developmental deficiencies in children.

    Facultative classes - Student will complete one subject in each of the following three sets and complete five lessons under the direction of an academic teacher. The three sets are: (1) Artistic-fine arts, music, children's theater, dance, or technical classes; (2) physical education - tourism and sightseeing, gymnastics, corrective gymnastics, or sports; and (3) Extralessons and Extraschool Work Methodology - work of circles of interest, work of club room, and work of youth organizations.

These three sets of facultative classes are exemplary ones. The availability of qualified faculty and local conditions will determine which classes will be available to students.

Monographic lecture - a system of individual lectures by professors on topics which stress a particular problem. The history of Polish Education would be one example.

Graduate's seminar - MA thesis seminars as candidate must prepare a thesis under this program.

Foreign language is optional. A student may take a foreign language during the first two years and may continue it during this program.

University or College - This program prepares teachers for service at the kindergarten, primary, lycea, and secondary technical levels. Candidates complete a five year program in one academic discipline, graduate without writing a thesis, or graduate with the MA degree.

Education of Special School Teachers

Training programs for special education teachers in Poland follow one of two basic forms of study. First, are programs centering on the needs of special schools including rehabilitation of invalids (mentally handicapped, deaf and hard of hearing, blind and dimsighted, and chronically ill and disabled). Second, are specialities useful for teachers who work at special schools and centers.

This study may be postgraduate study or for educators who have had no previous preparation in special education.

The following chart provides the syllabus of the special education program at Warsaw University.

SYLLABUS OF SPECIAL EDUCATION
WARSAW UNIVERSITY

Year	Content
I	BASIC SUBJECTS: History of basic psychology, logic, general psychology, political economy, propedeutic to education, biomedical basis of education, languages.
II	BASIC SUBJECTS: Modern philosophy, developmental psychology, history of education, sociology of education.
III	BASIC SUBJECTS: Political science, clinical psychology, theory of moral education, didactic.

III   Special education classes for 15 hours of
        lectures, 45 hours of seminars, and 15 hours
        of direct work with a handi-capped child.

        At year IV, special education students must
        choose one area of specialization. The areas
        are: adult education, education in cultural
        activities, care education, or special educa-
        tion.

IV   Student attends other classes such as in com-
        parative education, but must attend lectures
        and seminars depending upon area of speciali-
        zation.

        Adult education: Theory of Special
        Education, 12 hours lectures, 20 hours semi-
        nar.

        Education in Cultural Activities:
        Psychological Problems of Rehabilitation and
        special education, 20 hours lectures, 30
        hours seminar.

        Care Education: Preorientation and
        vocational guidance, 10 hours lecture, 30
        hours seminar.

        Special Education: diagnosis, 20 hours
        lecture, 40 hours seminar.

        All special education students also complete:

Individual and Social Skill of the Disabled, 100 hours of seminar and practice.

Note: During Year IV the following also apply:

*Each student chooses one or two additional subjects of individual interest, 90 hours.

*During Semester, I of Year IV, students who are specializing in special education, start writing their Masters Thesis. For Semesters, I & II, of years IV and V, they attend 2 hours each week for thesis seminars. Totals to 120 hours in the two years.

V   Semester I - Practice at a special school or other special education institution.

Semester II - Theory of Special Education, 4 hours lecture, 10 hours seminar. Therapeutic value of recreation and cultural activities, 15 hours seminar. Social Policy and Social Services for the Disabled, 40 hours seminar.

Note: The Master's Degree examinations conclude the program with a discussion over submitted thesis and an examination over special education. (Hulek. "Training of Personnel for Special Education")

Poland and other European countries have trained teachers in a vertical manner for each specific disability. Warsaw University has chosen to prepare in wide profile. Their graduates are not specialists in teaching children with a specific disability, but gain knowledge and practical skills across the whole region of special education. The student gains specific qualifications at the institution. After completing university studies, specialists from the Institute for Upgrading of Teachers Qualifications guide and instruct newly employed persons on the job. It is the belief of the special education faculty at Warsaw University, that training teachers in the wide profile and upgrading their qualifications at the work place is the current solution.

During the 1960's, special education candidates came from among regular practicing school teachers. Today, many candidates come from graduates of secondary schools. They also come from the ranks of or general and vocational schools. Many of the candidates have no

background in teaching, hence the need for program
change. The current practice is to recruit candidates
from among the pool of practicing classroom teachers.
Mainstreaming is making rapid progress in Polish
schools. Candidates for the teaching profession receive fifteen hours of lecture and forty-five hours of
seminar in mainstreaming. This will help the development and acceptance of mainstreaming within Polish
schools.

The Polish Teacher's Association

     The Polish Teacher's Association, founded in 1905,
is one of the oldest trade unions in Poland. The
Association is one of the largest unions with over
600,000 members. Personnel from all areas of education may become a member. Most Polish trade unions
only accept members from a small federation or classi-
fication of workers.

     The Association has an organization at national,
state, county, and individual school levels. Officers
are chosen by secret ballot for a four year term and
may run for a second four year term. After the eight
year term, a person may stand as a candidate for a
different office with the organization.

     On the national level, one hundred four members
are chosen. Forty-nine come from the state level with
one person per state and fifty-five members at-large.
A seventeen member steering committee is chosen from
the total members at the national level. A president
and two deputies, who may be chosen for a total of
eight years, operate national headquarters in Warsaw.
(Dr. Jan Zaciura, personal interview, 25 April
1989)

     The Association operates four enterprises to gener-
ate income for the Association. The projects are:

          1.   Vacation homes - Six medical treatment
               sanitariums and twelve vacation homes in
               various areas of Poland, are available
               to members for a small cost.

          2.   Extra Paid Education Activities - Camps
               are available year round for students in
               music, dance, and foreign language.
               Teachers and the Association receive
               extra pay.

3.   Tourist Bureau - In the last five years, a variety of excursions within and outside of Poland were available to the members. Members receive a reduced rate, but non-members may attend for a higher fee. During 1988, 30,000 people traveled within Poland, and 10,000 visitors came from other countries to Poland.

4.   Publishing House - The Association publishes a variety of materials. Some representative publications are eight instructional journals published at various levels. Examples include <u>Education Movement</u>, a weekly <u>Teacher's Voice</u>, and other timely materials. Due to the shortage of paper and rising printing costs, it is difficult to turn a profit.

The main part of the Association's program stresses educational activity.

The officers express concern that they want to become more than a trade union. The officers want to become a professional education organization.

Three key issues the Association attempts to influence are:

1.   Economics and school system operations

2.   Teaching and Teacher In-Service

3.   School administration and management.

An important concern is the young beginning teacher. During the first few years, the Association provides an informal organization to help the person into the job. They help secure a flat, and work with salary concerns. In addition, techniques for survival and support in-service is available to the beginning teacher.

During the first three years, a teacher serves a probationary period and during this time they are subject to release. During the fourth year, a teacher is nominated and examined. Automatic tenure is possible if the committee does not examine the teacher. A district level commission handles the examination process. The commission meets at least one time where they administer a written examination, and see a lesson taught by the teacher. After the lesson, the Committee talks with the teacher to provide feedback.

During the fifth year, a teacher undergoes regular examination to determine the proper level. Three levels may be utilized to raise teacher salaries and as an incentive for teachers to take additional education. The first level is without a MA degree. Level two the teacher must have a MA degree, and level three requires postgraduate work and publication of articles in educational journals.

The teacher evaluation process starts first within the school with an estimation of work from the Headmaster. Next a state commission examines for levels one and two. The process culminates with an examination by the National Commission in Warsaw.

Candidates meet the following criteria:

1.   a university graduate,

2.   have five years work experience,

3.   highest evaluation/opinion by the administrator and an A or B on the demonstration lesson,

4.   Commission sees a classroom lesson, conducts a discussion with the candidate over the lesson and takes a theoretical examination on discipline educational knowledge and the demonstration lesson.

The committee is comprised of a university professor, with other members. These members include one from the Center for Improvement of Teachers, and one teacher from the same subject area, but from a different school. The Committee also has a superior teacher from the state and the school's Headmaster.

Minimum time requirement and salary increase for each level is:

1st level - 5 years in teaching - 4,500Z

2nd level - 10 years in teaching - 5,500Z

3rd level - 15 years in teaching - 7,500Z

There is no restriction as to how many teachers may apply. Some candidates do not receive a level request, but are free to apply the next year. About fifty to sixty percent of the candidates receive level increases. About 30,000 teachers (seven percent of all Polish teachers) attain one of the three levels.

The Polish Teacher's Association negotiate salary with the national government. During the past few years, adjustments have been difficult to arrange due to a high rate of inflation.

A university degree, years of experience, and level of specialization   determine the teacher salary schedule.   Salaries are difficult to interpret as they may not be reliable due to the reporting system used by the government.   Fluctuations in the currency exchange rate often intensify the problem.

The average teacher salary during September, 1988 was 57,000 złotys. However, personnel in the produc-tivity sector salary average was 85,000 złotys.   In January 1989, teachers were to receive an increase to 90,000 złotys.

It is difficult to secure teachers for service in the villages and rural areas of Poland. These teachers receive ten percent over base salary and a free flat if available.   Current estimates place a shortage of 50,000 flats needed for teachers!

CHAPTER 6

PARENTAL VIEWS OF EDUCATION

Parents of children the world around hold a variety of opinions and views concerning the education their children should receive. Polish parents are no different. Interviewed parents shared their feelings and expressed hopes for their children. The parents shared strengths and weaknesses in the Polish educational system.

Homework

Teachers in the schools assign homework and expect that students will do the homework. During the first part of each class period the teacher scrutinizes each students' homework and the results entered in a grade book. Certainly the amount of homework will vary from teacher to teacher, grade level to grade level, and from subject to subject. In general, students in Poland devote from two to four hours per night on homework. Students often simply memorize the material. Younger students do not devote as much time to homework as are the older students. There are many good students in Poland who want to do well by achieving good grades. They are willing to spend many hours per night on their lessons. However, there is a very large and growing number of students who have little interest in schooling and so have little interest in completing homework assignments.

Do Polish parents help their children complete their homework? All parents interviewed with a resounding answer of yes. Parents seem to be eager to help, especially in the difficult areas or programs. Parents are aware that the classroom teacher usually has many pupils and that the pupils come from all types of environments. Parents must help their children at home. However, parents must teach at home because the teacher does not teach at school. One parent said, "I believe most parents, at least the ones

I know, do help their children with their homework. Yes, we spend what time is necessary to help each one of our children. We want them to learn and do well. Teachers do not teach, so we have to do it." (Dakowski, 1989)

Time is often the key factor, and with many Polish parents simply not having enough. Most parents are trying to survive from day to day. The pressures of job(s), daily standing and waiting in lines, necessary work at home, and daily meal preparation, are often overwhelming. The country's constant economic problems often become too much, and the parent often cannot help the child.

Favorite Teachers

Polish students have no difficulty in identifying their favorite teachers. These teachers exhibited characteristics such as; a demanding teacher, knowledge of subject matter, use of humor, and an up-to-date approach to teaching. In addition, favorite teachers maintain good relationships with the students and organize extra activities for their students.

Favorite Subjects

Favorite subjects in school varied from student to student and often were parallel with their favorite teacher. History, geography, math, drawing (art), writing type activities, physical fitness, chemistry, biology, and Polish literature were favorite subjects.

Strengths

Parents were able to identify some strengths of their schools. The system is traditional in which students can master cognitive knowledge. This was especially clear in areas of history, geography (place location, countries, mountains, capitals), and politics. Polish schools are good at encouraging memory development through this cognitive work load. (Falkowska, 1989)

The feeling seems to exist that the schools are perfect for the average child. Job schools (vocational schools) are another strength of the Polish educational system.

Weaknesses

Weaknesses within the Polish educational system were quick to surface. Parents were now aware of many attributes now missing or lacking for their children.

Physical facilities, the actual classrooms, are in extremely short supply in Poland. (For additional information see Chapter 8, Committee for National Education.)

In general, there are too few school buildings lacking proper equipment, but with an over-abundance of pupils. Classes often have forty pupils per class. Therefore, overcrowding occurs and most schools operate one, two, or even three shifts of students and faculty each day. Parents become very frustrated in trying to cope with students' timetables. Starting and ending times vary from grade level to grade level. Often, children in the same family attend several schools, each with different schedules. Safety hazards often exist because of improperly installed and maintained school equipment.

Teachers in Poland are underpaid, tired, and often overworked. Low salary has been one reason why many university students choose not to become teachers. As a result, the qualified and dedicated individuals choose not to teach. In addition, there is a problem of having the same teacher stay the whole school year in the same classroom. Teachers often change and go from one classroom assignment to another throughout the year, resulting in problems for the children and their parents.

Parents do not view teachers with high esteem. Consistently, they feel teachers really do not do any teaching in their classrooms. Said one parent, "We feel all the teacher does is to assign a block of work or material to be completed for the next day. It's up to the student to complete the work at home that night and go to school the next day where they give back the material. The teacher, after checking the homework, promptly assigns another block for the next day, and so on and on." (Dakowski, 1989)

Two polarized views of education seem to be developing within the country. In one position, parents

are angry with the schools and teachers because they
teach too much at school and home. Students receive a
certificate for little or no work. An opposite view is
that schools are teaching too much of what parents feel
is unimportant. Therefore, they want the schools to
teach only specialized bodies of knowledge and skills.
These parents feel that quality of education is low
and, suggest private education as an answer. (See
Chapter 7 for additional information).

Today in Poland, the intelligentsia (an unofficially recognized class of articulate persons devoted
to intellectual, cultural, and social matters), is
realizing more and more that the nation's schools
cannot adequately carry out their proper function.
Individual parents are now deciding to take charge of
the education of their children. Parents decide about
the profession their child should pursue and then
devise a variety of tracks to accomplish this goal.

Special Elite Track

            Vacation   School

                        HOME

            Travel   Personal Computers

The parent will use any avenue to help the child
achieve the parents' professional goal.

General Comments

Report cards need improvement to provide more
information to parents. This problem shows the general
lack of communication and information between parents
and schools.

Sports, arts, and music are lacking or receive
little stress in school. Parents do not trust the
schools and the schools do not trust the parents.

Teachers do not like school and children. Pupils
often see teachers as not being fair. Inconsistency
occurs between what teachers say and what they do. The
basic reason is the Communist control and censorship
which causes confusion in actual life. In general, the
school day is a tiresome routine. Parents feel teachers make too many demands on students and do not provide a helpful classroom environment. It is felt

teachers do not look at students as people and do not take the time to get to know them as individuals. (Adamowicz, 1989)

There seems to be many people without proper educational qualifications who teach in Poland. The Expert Committee for National Education estimate as many as 40,000 teachers lack proper qualifications. Parents reported children often knew as much or more than their teachers. There seems to exist a special problem in the elementary schools. Often principals and staff, by their actions, show they do not like children or like being with them.

Teachers now teach to the middle group of students. Therefore, top students receive little challenge and low students still may not understand the material.

In former times, teachers held god-like status, but today too much negative discussion occurs at home about the teacher. It is usually criticism the student hears and so upon entering school he or she has a bad outlook about the teacher.

Some teachers do not serve as good role models. A gap often occurs between what teachers say and what teachers actually do.

Poland has survived many educational changes, but little has been done actually to improve the schools. (Welbel,1989)   Parents feel so much money is appropriated on the changes, plans formulated, then put into practice, only to find a lack of buildings, teachers, and money. Real needs do not match actual needs of the country. The needs are theoretical and do not reflect real changes. An example was the proposed ten year obligatory school which would extend schooling two years beyond the current eight years. Work started, some money was given for the project, but the scheme did not work and abandoned due to no money. The point is that the people really need to want these changes and not simply changes proposed by governmental leaders.

CHAPTER 7

GENERAL INFORMATION

Private Schools

One result from Round Table discussions between Government and leaders of Solidarity in the spring 1989, teachers and parents can set up private (social) schools. The Polish court system approved the Social Educational Association. The central aim of this organization is not to improve existing schools, but to create new schools.

Under provisions of the agreement, the new schools would have power to hire teachers and pay a higher salary than is possible under the State system. Further, the schools must locate suitable buildings as they would not be able to secure regular State buildings. This is a formidable problem since physical facilities are scarce. Class size would remain ten to fifteen pupils per class. This is much lower than current pupil and teacher ratio in State operated schools. However, the private schools will follow the regular State mandated curriculum. Better results from teaching will be possible due to changes in methods and organization. Since regular State schools are stressful places for students, and as a result students are nervous in this environment, private schools will remove the stress.

Tuition would range from forty to fifty thousand złoty per month per child. Scholarships will be available for poorer students. Opponents say a negative selection process will operate where only children from parents who can pay the tuition will be able to attend.

People are positive to the approach which they feel will break the monopoly, the Socialist system has over education. Parents maintain a wait-and-see attitude as they need to see an actual private operation.

Poland has fourteen general high schools operated by the Roman Catholic Church. The State mandated curriculum and separate instruction is available for boys and girls. In addition, PAX, a Christian Association, operates an all male high school in Warsaw. This school also follows the State mandated curriculum. The Liceum im. K. Gorski is a State experimental school in Warsaw. It has been able to function because of the personality and strength of its director. Students must prove one area of excellence. Most students are from parents who serve as governmental leaders.

Country and Embassy Education

In Warsaw, four countries provide education, at various levels, for pupils. All schools have an embassy connection and secure funds from each country. Each country determines matters of curriculum and accreditation. These schools do not have to follow the Polish mandated curriculum. Polish students may attend schools sponsored by the United States of America, France, and Germany. Japan accepts only Japanese students in their school.

American School-Grades K-9. Students must complete high school in another country, Great Britain. Funds come from the United States State Department. Tuition charges are $6,000.00 per year, per child.

French School-Grades Pre-Kindergarten-High School.

German School-Grades Pre-Kindergarten up to level for high school entrance examination.

Open Studies

During 1979, several faculty members who taught at Warsaw University came to a conclusion. The conclusion was why not open the university to anyone who wanted to study? Some faculty members were growing tired of working with regular, eighteen to twenty-five year old, unmotivated students. They decided to work with more motivated people who wanted to discover and experience a joy of learning. Zofia Blanka Sokolewicz (personal interview 4 May 1989.)

Four faculty members (Theoretical Physics, Biology, Art Pedagogy, and Sociology) prepared the initial request and program. Then the wait began and the wait

lasted for ten years! Governmental officials seemed
annoyed at the request and raised a variety of questions about the proposal. Who would receive instruction? What teaching methods would they use? Where
would they secure teaching materials? Who would do the
teaching? Why would university faculty want to work
with these students? Who would pay for this project?
Questions continued to flow and answers continued to
flow and finally approval was given during the 1988
academic year.

After preliminary planning, the teachers decided
to hold a general meeting to allow "new students" a
chance to talk and discuss possible programs. After
the discussion, several programs and offerings emerged.
The teachers decided to use a variety of teaching
techniques, such as lecture, discussion groups, experimental learning, field trips, and audio-visuals.

Four courses emerged: 1.) Myth and Mythical Thinking; 2.) Beauty; 3.) Man and Environment; and 4.) Fear
and Courage. Teachers had to be recruited, classes
advertised, people arrived and had to be broken into
groups. Instructors found many of the students shy and
unable to verbalize what they wanted to study. Some
students listened to the whole lecture while other
students wanted to have personal contact with a tutor.
One-half of the students decided not to attend classes,
a cadre of students remained.

These students meet every second Saturday for a
four hour period. Often the participants would decide
to meet for a longer period of time, and some groups
decided to meet every Saturday. A variety of people
from ages eighteen to eighty two attended. Students
come from the Warsaw area with some students as far
away as 300 kilometers (180 miles) to attend.

Student needs provided a base for special lectures. Psychology and Ethics were extremely popular
with the open studies students. No doubt this stemmed
from problems students were experiencing in their daily
lives. An opportunity was given for students to ask
questions with an opportunity for solving the problems.

Faculty members report they wish to change from
regular teaching appointments to a teaching assignment
in the open university. The Minister of Education and
the Rector (President) of the University are deciding

staffing for future years.

Universities in Cracow and Poznań have similar programs. The Cracow program is a four-year, structured, general education program.

Students ask for selected courses to be offered again and, ask for new course offerings. Included are: Medicine and Alternative Medicine, Health and Disease, Man and Woman, Polish History and Literature, European History and Literature, Human Rights, and Ethnic Minorities.

Results from the students are encouraging. They report liking the classes and the opportunity to study at the university which was once only a dream. Perhaps the open studies program will become a hidden revolution.

Świetlica

Most Polish women work professionally outside the home. One result is they have less and less time to look after their children. Polish schools are helping solve the dilemma of the working parents. What should we do with our children before and after lessons at the primary school? Świetlica is the answer. Bonota Zawada (class interview 1989.)

Primary schools located in large cities and urban areas, provide Świetlica. Often Świetlica's are not available in farm and out-lying rural areas in Poland.

Children in grades one, two, and three attend Świetlica. Older children are responsible to be on their own before and after lessons and until parents return home. In limited cases, a parent may request older children to also stay in the class. In actual practice, older students simply are free with little supervision and as a result often form gangs.

At the beginning of the school year, parents complete an application form providing general family and financial information. Governmental funds, scholarships, or lunches are given to children who have poor parents or come from an alcoholic family.

Teachers operate Świetlica from 7 A.M. until 5 P.M. Children may spend several hours in the morning if classes do not start until 10 or 11 A.M. and could stay after the conclusion of lessons in the afternoon. The parents or some other family member usually pick the child up from school. Parents, may also give permission for the child to leave school alone and return home.

Cost of the program varies from school to school, with a symbolic fee of 500 złotys per child, per day usually charged. Lunches are not free, except for poor children, and they cost about 180 złotys each. Children usually sleep and rest after lunch.

Teachers who work in Świetlica receive special training for this work and work twenty-six hours per week. This compares to an average, full time classroom teacher, who would teach for eighteen hours per week.

Typically a child would go four hours per day. Teachers determine the time schedule for activities. Activities include homework, outside play time during good weather, reading books, and playing games. Other activities include circles of interest such as amateur theater which stages plays for other children, dance and art activities.

Świetlica is a very good way of helping working parents and organizing pupil's time in an interesting way. Teachers are available for extra help with homework and problems of the child. Świetlica is extremely popular with parents since the cost is reasonable and they can be sure children are not roaming the streets unattended.

Computers in Education

The use of computers in education in Poland is limited by their availability. Dr. Krysztof Kruszewski (personal interview 29 March 1989.)

Computers are available in some schools in the Mathematics and Science track, within General Secondary Schools, located in urban areas. However, rarely are computers and the teaching process integrated. Computers would seldom be available in primary schools.

Computer problems are one of cost, availability of hardware and software, and language problems. Since most computer programs are written in English, an immediate problem exists for many Poles. Computers may indirectly cause more Poles to learn English and English may be a motivator to use computers.

The University of Warsaw Department of Education has two computers. One was a gift from a West German company and the other had to be purchased. They are utilized for administrative tasks, word processing and additional minor uses. These computers are not for instructional purposes. No computer classes are available for students.

The use of computers often has been for playing games and not for serious instructional purposes. Some parents are taking more control of the education of their children (See Chapter 6-Parental View of Education) and are providing computers and software for their children's use. In urban areas, few private computer clubs are available.

Business firms make limited use of computers. Examples of computer use in business are auto parts are ordered from West Germany and railroad reservations are ordered and tickets printed by computer. Change is coming and so the future of computer usage in Poland is bright.

Official Grading System

The official grading system in effect from grades one through secondary school is as follows:

> 5 - The best grade - Very good.
> 4 - Good
> 3 - Average, enough work
> 2 - Below average, not enough work

Unofficially, teachers will issue pluses or minuses.

Promotion

If a student does not do well, they still receive a school certificate for the year. Promotion is not given if the student has 2's on their report card. School personnel are interested in keeping the number of non-promotions low. Each school has a Pedagogical Council to approve promotions and retentions. Often the council will hand out a promotion even if a student has received one 2 for the year. In grades four through eight, a student may, during a holiday period, make up poor work. The teacher then administers a special examination and may alter the original grade.

Parent Immigration to Another Country

Poles will often immigrate to another country. When one parent (usually male) goes abroad, often they do not return. The female is then left at home with the child. Teachers often have problems with these children in class.

School Certificate for Grade Three

(See following pages for a sample certificate.)

Szkoła Podstawowa Nr 103
im. Bohaterów Warszawy 1939 - 1945
w Warszawie
u l. .... (pełna nazwa i adres szkoły)
tel. 42-24-55

ŚWIADECTWO SZKOLNE

DLA UCZNIÓW KLAS II i III SZKOŁY PODSTAWOWEJ

Anna   Mieszalska

(Imię i nazwisko)

urodzon*a* dnia *28 września*   19*77* r.

w *Warszawie*   woj. ————————

uczęszczał*a* w roku szkolnym 19*86/87* do klasy *trzeciej*
(słownie)

Szkoły Podstawowej Nr *103* im. *Bohaterów*

Warszawy   1939 - 1945

w *Warszawie*   woj. ————————

i uchwałą Rady Pedagogicznej z dnia *22 czerwca*

———— otrzymał*a* promocj*ę* do klasy *czwartej*
(słownie)

Warszawa, dnia *26 czerwca* 19*87* r.

Nr *19*   DYREKTOR SZKOŁY

mgr ....

Min. Ośw. i W. 03-14-11/352 —
Zam. 3612 Wyd. Akc. Pn — PZGMK-4 77393 86 — 1.384.600 — pism. III/80

The narrow dark line on front signifies best academic effort. A limited number may be given in each class.

ŚWIADECTWO SZKOLNE

Anne Mieszafske
(imię i nazwisko)

urodzon___ ___ia _28 unejma_ 19 _77_ r.

w _____awie_ woj. _—_

uczeszcza___ w roku szkolnym 19 _87/88_ do klasy _cuvarfaj_
(słowne)

Szkoły P_____owej _____ Nr _103_

im. _____terós —Varnacy_

w _____avie_ woj. _—_

i uchwałą ___y Pedagogicznej z dnia _20 cierpca 1788_

___trzymał _a_ promocję z wyróżnieniem

do klasy _piafaj_
(słowne)

_____se_, dnia _24. 06_ 19 _88_ r.

Nr _1.___

DYREKTOR SZKOŁY

Mgr J Trepkiwta

Min. Ośw. i W. ___ W
Zam. 3615 Wy___ — PZGMK — 75568/88 — 476920 — paźm. III/80

Anna Mieszalska
(imię i nazwisko)

otrzymał **a** w klasie *trzeciej* następujące oceny roczne:
(słownie)

zachowanie — Behavior	*wzorowe*
język polski — Political Language.	*bardzo dobry*
środowisko społeczno-przyrodnicze. Social & Natural Environment	*bardzo dobry*
matematyka Mathematics	*bardzo dobry*
plastyka Painting & Drawing	*bardzo dobry*
muzyka Music	*bardzo dobry*
praca-technika Manual Work	*bardzo dobry*
kultura fizyczna Physical Education	*bardzo dobry*

Szczególne osiągnięcia w zakresie:

Opuścił **a** w roku szkolnym _18_ dni nauki,
w tym nie usprawiedliwiono _1_

WYCHOWAWCA KLASY

Skala ocen:
a) wyników nauki: bardzo dobry, dobry, dostateczny, niedostateczny.
b) zachowania: wzorowe, wyróżniające, poprawne, nieodpowiednie, naganne.

Otrzymał _e_ w klasie _czwartej_ następujące oceny roczne
(słownie)

zachowanie	*wzorowe*
Behavior	
język polski	*bardzo dobry*
Political Language	
język rosyjski	—
Russian	
język	—
Foreign Language	*bardzo dobry*
historia	
History	—
wiedza o społeczeństwie	
Knowledge about Society	*bardzo dobry*
biologia z higieną	
Biology with Hygiene	*bardzo dobry*
geografia	
Geography	—
fizyka z astronomią	
Physics & Astronomy	*bardzo dobry*
matematyka	
Mathematics	—
chemia	
Chemistry	*bardzo dobry*
plastyka	
Painting & Drawing	*bardzo dobry*
muzyka	
Music	*bardzo dobry*
praca—technika	
Manual Work	—
praktyki uczniowskie	
Pupil's Practice	*bardzo dobry*
kultura fizyczna	—
Physical Education	
przysposobienie obronne	
Preparation for Defense	

Przedmioty nadobowiązkowe

Szczególne osiągnięcia:

Opuścił _e_ w roku szkolnym _145_ godzin lekcyjnych,
w tym nie usprawiedliwiono _—_

WYCHOWAWCA KLAS

mgr *Olenek*

Skala ocen:
　a) wyników nauki: bardzo dobry, dobry, dostateczny, niedostateczny.
　b) zachowania: wzorowe, wyróżniające, poprawne, nieodpowiednie, naganne

Drugs, Alcohol, and Sexually Transmitted Diseases

Drugs, alcohol, and sexually transmitted diseases
are a serious problem in the Polish society. Drugs are
a problem mainly with young people, but alcohol and
sexually transmitted diseases are also of concern to
older people. Alcohol consumption is very extensive in
Poland with little help given by governmental policies.
The government tries to deal with the drug problem, but
is silent concerning alcohol and venereal disease.
People want to solve these problems, but in practice do
little and often move toward a point of no return.

The young generation in Poland has acquired a new
addiction, that to drugs. The problem is not as extensive in numbers, as in other societies, but the Polish
society and government need to pay heed to the situation. There are many motivations to use drugs. At
first it is an experiment, the desire to try something
new, which often turns into addiction. One person
(Andrzej Zuk, class interview 1989) recounts meeting a
young person who asked for a small amount of money to
buy a train ticket. She returned a few minutes later
to ask for money once again. Sexual service is often
offered in exchange for money. The money is used to
purchase drugs.

The older generations have escaped drug addiction,
but for a long time they have been under another addiction, alcohol. The drinking of all kinds of alcohol
has been a long tradition in Poland, but seemed to get
out of hand after World War II. Many other nations in
Europe consume large quantities of alcohol. Drinking is
often a part of social events, dinner, and an addition
to the atmosphere. In Poland, drinking vodka, beer, or
wine is an event or occasion itself. It is the actual
aim of parties, meetings, or visits. Therefore, long
lines form in front of liquor shops daily and especially before weekends. Alcoholism is and will continue to
be a problem in Polish society.

The young people in Poland are also very heavily
into alcohol. One young man remembers that liquor was
available at every party he attended. Drinking became
essential to have a good time, to relax, and to make
contact with others. Drinking is found in all levels
of society with few examples of non-drinkers. Many
students who find themselves in the company of alcohol
users, are often forced to drink, thereby not being

alienated or regarded as some sort of a freak. Alcohol
seems to have overwhelmed the country as it has become
one of the favorite past times of many Poles.

     Several reasons   explain Poland's high alcoholic
consumption.   One reason is the tradition of drinking.
However, this tradition has gone far beyond European
norms of drinking. Young people in Poland start to
drink at a very early age with students in the primary
school consuming liquor.   Eleven and twelve year olds
are consuming alcohol.   Adults drink and so young
people model their behavior.   Another reason is governmental policies.   Official programs exist which try to
lower alcohol consumption, but in practice not much
change is made.   Since the alcohol industry is a
source of major revenue for the government, not much
will be done to reduce the needed revenue.   Prices have
increased, but consumption has not decreased.   Many
shops in every town sell alcohol.   Illegal alcohol is
often available in closed shops, in the right shops, or
in private homes.

     Sexually transmitted diseases are of concern to
the government.   Several venereal disease clinics exist
in Poland.   They provide limited information, but here
efforts end.   Condoms, which offer the simplest kind of
protection against sexually transmitted diseases, are
difficult to buy.

     There is public opinion against alcoholism, drug
addiction, and the spreading of venereal diseases.
However, people themselves often add to these problems.
There is a general feeling in Poland that a non-drinker
is different and is separated from society.   Most
Polish youth find there is not much for them to do in
the evenings. Warsaw has some forms of entertainment,
but in other cities entertainment is still lacking. One
would not spend the whole evening every day at movies,
theaters, and ballets.   Evening parties and disco-
theques serve alcohol.   There is also a tendency to
escape the daily activities and the easiest way is to
get drunk.

     The problems seem to go along with the overall
atmosphere in Polish society, with the economic situation, and a feeling of certain hopelessness.   This
pattern may cause a complete downfall of the whole
nation if immediate action is not taken.

Aids, Pregnancy, and Cigarettes in Polish Schools

AIDS, pregnancy and cigarette smoking are among the most important problems teachers face in Polish schools. The significance and source of each problem is different. Therefore, each problem will be treated separately.

Cigarette smoking was a serious offense in the grammar and secondary schools about twenty years ago. During the 1980's, the feeling existed that cigarette smoking was something that was very difficult to control. According to the law, persons age sixteen or older may purchase cigarettes. Often these persons are still in grammar school. Ten and twelve year olds are securing cigarettes as the age limit is often ignored. School authorities usually follow the principle of trying to combat smoking in the schools.

Smoking rooms were made available in secondary schools. At first this was a shocking move, but accepted as common place today. The result was a slow decrease in the number of young smokers. Students found that smoking was not as fascinating as they thought. However, teenagers consider smoking as an attribute of maturity. The peer group influences ideas about smoking and often smoking became fashionable and not an addiction. One teacher reports that most young smokers do not like the habit, but their attitude towards cigarettes exists out of the fear of other teenager's opinions. These occasional smokers often do become heavy adult smokers.

Pregnancy of young women is a far more serious problem. Though the scale of pregnancy is fewer, in each case of a teenager's pregnancy, there is no doubt a life tragedy for both the girl and usually for her parents. The reasons are due to the lack of information and the very primitive and prudish attitudes toward sexual problems of young people. These attitudes are often held by both teachers and parents. Modern forms of contraception are not readily available to the average person.

The real problems start with the unwanted pregnancy. The school administrators and teachers must cope with strong pressure from the pregnant girl's school friends and their parents. They usually demand the removal of the girl from the school environment as it is felt her presence immoral for the rest of the pupils.   Often the girl is under intense pressure from her former friends, parents, and teachers who must work under the pressure of the public opinion attacks. That is why it often happens that a young girl who realizes all the possible problems she is facing, decides to avoid them and chooses suicide as a way out of the problems.

Government reports confirm the increase in the number of pregnancies every year. The teenagers are fully mature from a sexual standpoint, but still lack from a psychological and responsibility standpoint. In addition, they can not rely on help from the adults around them, and that is why the first pregnancy is often the last one.

The number of school age pupils with AIDS is very small. Though the problem is not yet a crucial one, Polish schools, administrators, and teachers must prepare to face the disease both from the organizational and informational point of view. As teachers are unable to help inform teenagers about sexual problems, there are no specialists who can warn the young pupils of the AIDS danger. There was a case of a boy in one of Warsaw's schools whose father was an AIDS carrier. The boy was not given admission to the school.

CHAPTER 8
COMMITTEE FOR NATIONAL EDUCATION

During February 1987, the Government established a committee of thirty-four people called the Expert Committee for National Education. Six members were not active and so resigned, leaving twenty-eight members to carry out the task. Professor Dr. hab. Czesław Kupisiewicz of Warsaw University, chaired the committee. Czesław Kupisiewicz (personal interview, 21 April 1989) Professor Kupisiewicz has had a wide variety of teaching experience at primary, secondary, and vocational levels. He has also had experience with teacher training, Warsaw University, and worked at the Polish Academy of Sciences. Further, he had served as chair of the previous two expert committees. The 1973 committee was under the sponsorship of the Ministry of Education and the 1979 committee by the Polish Academy of Sciences.

The Committee had two major tasks. First, they were to conduct a diagnosis of the current Polish education system. Second, they were to develop proposals, with guidelines, for future development in education.

The Committee worked for a two year period, completing its final report in July 1989. The final report included thirteen sub-parts such as a comparative evaluation of the Polish Educational system, and state of health of pupils. Also included were pre-school education and its development, primary schools, secondary schools, and higher education. After a diagnosis the report concluded with three future outlines: 1.)stagnation, 2.)animation, and 3.)development. Development meant maintaining present educational levels with some modest increases.

In the process of diagnosis of the Polish Educational System four areas deserve special attention.

Teachers: More than 100,000 teachers in elementary Polish schools lack the proper preparation to teach. In addition, about 6-10,000 qualified teachers leave the profession each year. This outward movement occurs due to years of poor pay and inadequate living conditions. These factors then result in negative selection of candidates who select education as a future profession.

Facilities: 5,000 new school buildings, containing 100,000 classrooms at the elementary and secondary levels are now needed to have enough facilities. In addition, 10,000 present school buildings need major repairs. About 40 percent of these schools in need of repairs are in general and vocational areas. The state of the economy is so extremely precarious that the school infrastructure would find it difficult to fulfill these needs. To further exacerbate this facility dilemma, the number of students in schools continues to increase.

Low Scholastic Standings: In 1988, fifty percent of kindergarten pupils could actually attend schools in Poland. Forty-three percent of pupils finishing primary schools could study in secondary schools. Out of the forty-three percent, less than twenty percent enrolled in general education schools. This is a distinct problem because most university students come from general education schools.

Ten percent of students leaving secondary schools study at higher educational institutions. As a result, Poland has a low number of academic school graduates per 10,000 inhabitants. Poland is only ahead of East Germany and Rumania in the Socialist countries. Further, Poland remains well behind other countries of the world. These countries include Sweden, Soviet Union, France, Japan, United States, and the United Kingdom.

Quite clearly, these low scholastic standings do not correspond to the present or the future expected needs and aspirations of Polish society.

Educational Results: Results of education are lowest in the Polish primary schools. This is especially true in the lower grades, and in kindergarten. At these levels, there are over 40,000 teachers who are teaching without any course work in the art or science of teaching. One must be careful here because often these teachers are concurrently taking educational courses to gain qualifications. We know the crucial importance of education during these early years. During this formative period, pupil's attitudes toward school, school subjects, and feelings about themselves become manifest. Polish schools stress one-sided domination of intellectual education where students receive knowledge from books. Students only gain knowledge and reproduce information on tests. However, this practice has adversely affected pupils' emotional and volition development. Further, it has overburdened them with too many school lessons, especially those lessons which rely on rote memorization. Pupils do not like these stressful schools.

Let us now turn our attention to the three scenarios proposed by the Committee. The main problem is to be able to break the schools out of the structure, curriculum, and methods of teaching which have resulted in such an abysmal performance. All accounts depend upon the amount of money the Government will be able to provide. Therefore, the Committee states that in order for education to move forward in Poland, a fixed amount of the national income must go to education. The current level is 4.7 percent of the total national budget. The monies are for all levels of education and 1.0 percent for U-P-A-C education. Should these fixed rates decline, education in Poland would be in a state of catastrophe.

Scenario of Stagnation With Some Areas of Improvement:

The major theme is one of holding the present educational level constant while making minor improvements. This may be possible if the economy turns more favorably in Poland. Items would include: 1.) the financial conditions of teachers, 2.) the education of teachers (Teacher preparation exists under a variety of schools and this move would bring together the variety of teacher preparation programs), 3.) prepare teachers of mathematics, history, etc., instead of the current practice of creating mathematicians, historians, etc. This transition would cause a shift from subject-centered to student-centered preparation of teachers, 4.) shift from pupils simply receiving knowledge to becoming acquirers of knowledge, thinkers, and inquirers, and 5.) employment of additional teachers for projected increase in enrollment.

Scenario of Animation: Maintain Present Level With Some Modest Increase: The purpose would be to satisfy the demand for quantity education. Attempts to increase the percentage of pupils attending schools is necessary under this plan. Also change in the structure and change in the program of existing schools is necessary. Other plans would propose additional models, ie. a nine-year elementary school followed by a three-year secondary school. Some specific suggestions include: 1.) shorten the kindergarten from four to three years, 2.) where possible put kindergartens and early elementary school in an integrated curriculum manner, 3.) start children in school one year earlier than now, that is age six instead of seven for primary schools, 4.) combine some vocational programs, 5.) increase the number of youth attending secondary school and change the curriculum of educating for practical skills (such as shorthand, accounting, library science, gardening, and animal husbandry), 6.) create an open university system, and 7.) de-centralize educational administration and create school autonomy.

Development Scenario: The purpose of this would be to satisfy students' social educational needs and aspirations, both quantitatively and qualitatively. Public kindergartens, a widely accessible secondary school, and differentiated higher education for about twenty five percent of persons who have passed the examination. A modern system of open and permanent education, and cooperation between school and parent. The proposed school of the future would be quite different from the present one. One difference would have classes scheduled outside school hours where children would become more self-dependent in their thinking and acting. The educational process would take place more outside the school, such as in museums, work places, and public institutions.

A question remains as how to carry out and how to follow up on the proposed reforms. In achieving the proposed reforms, the following results are possible: 1.) a significant change and improvement in the training of teachers, 2.) enrichment of school resources which may allow organizational changes. This will also help to reduce the number of shifts of pupils at schools, 3.) increase the availability of kindergarten, secondary, and higher education schools, 4.) changes in school environments (move from negative feelings to positive feelings where pupils feel good and everybody feels good being with the pupils), and 5.) making schools more independent and cooperative institutions.

Committee members are recommending changes not by a wide, frontal attack, but almost in a checkerboard, school by school attack. It would be difficult to test or check on broad sweeping reforms. However, in a school by school approach, a much more careful analysis would be possible.

The received report awaits future action. (Edukacja Narodowym Priorytetem, 1989) An up-date on recent developments is in Chapter 9.

CHAPTER 9

BEYOND THE 1990's

Student Organizations (University Level)

Today there is a plethora of student organizations
at the university level. Some organizations have many
members, others have just a handful of members, and
still others have just a small organizational structure.

The two most forceful student organizations are
the Zrzeszenie Studentów Polskich (Z.S.P. - Polish
Student Organization) and the Niezalezny Zwiozek Studentów (Z.N.S. - Independent Student Organization).
Regardless of the organization, the message is clear
that Polish students are taking an active role in the
administration and operation of universities. Students
organize, elect representatives and send the representatives to attend educational meetings at all levels in
the university. Not only do they attend, they can
discuss and vote on all items. Voting on academic
degrees is the only exception.

1990 Update - Student Organizations (University Level)

Students are using the strike as a tactic to show
displeasure against proposed new education laws. The
students are striking because they want more votes in
the election of Rectors (Presidents) and Deans. In
addition, students also want more votes on all bodies
of the university.

In the discussion stage, there is even a proposal
which would place students on country-wide committees,
such as curriculum.

Teaching Religion in Schools

A crucial issue facing the new Polish government,

in the field of education, concerns teaching religion in the schools. It is a very complex issue with many sides to consider. In discussions with many people, no consensus seemed to emerge. Some positions did seem to be clear. However, other positions were vague and not as clearly stated. This illustrates the size of the winds of change which are sweeping across the Polish countryside. Winds are sometimes unpredictable, sometimes quiet, sometimes violent, and sometimes blowing forward. At other times winds sometimes blow backwards, sometimes cause stress, and sometimes sooth and reassure. No one seems to know which type is blowing today!

The Roman Catholic Church's position is for allowing religious training within the schools. Church leaders are fairly aggressive in this matter, but not pushy as they appear to support the current government. Not all people nor all priests favor this position. They feel it is a good system now since students do not associate religious training with the poor feelings they hold about schools. Perhaps students would see religion as just another course if taught in the schools.

The current governmental leaders believe that religious instruction should remain in the churches where it has been. If the Church can teach on school property, some leaders feel too much church influence will be present in the schools. Strong nationalistic feelings which stress Poles as Catholics and good Catholics as Poles seem to be emerging. Often these people lack good feelings toward ethic minorities, democracy, and toward western ideas. As a result, people may use the issue of teaching religion in the schools as a weapon to gain strength.

There are two other issues of concern to governmental education leaders. First, there is concern that other religious groups will want to teach their type of religion in the schools. Undue stress will then occur on schedules, curriculum and the use of physical facilities. Second, how should the government deal with the wishes of non-believers?

One Pole felt the teaching of religion in the schools is similar to the frontiers (border) question. Both issues were solved over the last forty to fifty years. New changes are coming about and in both cases to try a change back to what they used to be would be a disaster.

Legislation allowing religious lessons in schools gained approval in August 1990. Lessons might occur at the start of the day or after school. Non-believers would not have to attend lessons. Some private schools have declined to offer lessons in religion.

Religion

Today in Poland, other religions exist. Examples include Zen Buddhism, Hinduism, Islam's mystical version - Sufism, and a variety of occults.

One occult, the Polish Anthroposophic Society, is setting up several kindergartens and a school specifically to promote the anthroposophic pedagogical ideas. They have set up several dozen biodynamic farms that produce food without the use of any chemical agents. Further, an association coordinates their work and distributes their products.

The most significant social innovation might stem from the introduction of pluralism into the nation's mentality and lifestyle, a pluralism that is much needed in the post-communist development of Poland. The alternative to this road to development is contained in the slogan "Catholic-Pole," which strongly limits the areas of pluralism and sets us back from Europe and the world." (Tadeusz, 1990)

Expert Committee for National Education Reform

The report was written by a reform group of people living in a socialist oriented culture. The experts were people who were close to the passing government and at the end of the period of a Socialist country.

The conditions in Poland were such that no logical progress was possible and so there has been no public debate held on the report. Parliament has discussed the report and many legislators from the left say current government leaders are neglecting the report. On the other hand, the report does not fit the new reality, social, and political structures in 1990 Poland. Others react that the report is pendantic in nature. The document was good at describing conditions, but short on explanations. Others acknowledge it as a report, but will consider it at a future date. One educational leader, high in the current government,

says he has read the report, but asks how can I follow
it? He has stated he will accept the report and just
place it aside.

University

In the past, Polish students entered the university and continued to attend until completing the work to
the degree. Many students are now breaking their
studies at the university level to go overseas to study
and to make money. If students break their studies,
they may have to pay money for the longer study period
to the university. Of course, student organizations
opposed this move because they have had free education.
However, the chance still exists for the fees.

School Names Changed

One small way to illustrate change in Polish
schools of the 1990's, is the continuation of a movement that started in 1980's. Many school's patron
names were changed. Suddenly, revolutionists', and
communist activists' names were not used. Not only
have school names undergone change, but also street,
town, and monument names. This was the first symbolic
rejection of an imposed alien system that had never
really gained acceptance in Poland.

Foreign Language Teachers Needed

The new Polish government requires all students to
take a western foreign language and the process should
start in grade one, if possible. Therefore, in 1991
English is obligatory as early as possible. However,
there is a shortage of qualified teachers of foreign
language and that shortage is especially critical in
English. Current estimates place that shortage of
English teachers at twenty thousand. However, it is
not merely a matter of counting numbers, but one of new
ideology in the government.

In Białystok Wojewodztwo (state) twelve qualified
teachers of English are available and the need is for
one hundred fifty.

To meet this demand, the government is proposing
three-year English Teachers Colleges with a B.A. degree
without thesis. The main concern will be to prepare
teachers of English, not scholars. Candidates will

learn English and learn how to teach English as a subject.

There will be two types of English Teachers Colleges. One type will be within the existing structure of a university with graduates recciving a university diploma. The second type will be under the control of the local school level. The Kuratorium will issue their graduates a diploma similar to other post-secondary school graduates.

Three types of teachers will staff these colleges. First, Polish teachers with a MA or Ph.D. degree, with some training in teaching, will provide most of the instruction.   Second, American teachers from the Peace Corps will increase this cadre. Third, British teachers, from the Voluntary Service Overseas will further aid the colleges.

Expectations are that about one-half of the candidates for this college, would be Polish teachers who wished to re-train to secure a teaching position.

There is widespread interest and many candidates are applying for these new teaching positions. The admissions examination contains a test in English. Available facilities will determine the number of candidates who may enter the program.

In theory, students have a choice of foreign languages. However, in reality students do not have a choice because of a lack of teachers.

Reform of University Academic Ranks

The old system of academic ranks and titles (see Chapter 4 - Postgraduate Studies) has undergone change in the new education act. The changes are:

United States of America	Poland
M.A.	Student will enter and complete the M.A. degree.
Assistant Professor	Student will enter and complete post-graduate studies with the Ph.D. degree.
Associate Professor	Student will complete requirements for dr. hab (Doctor Habilitowany), but no longer use

                              the title docent.

Full Professor   Professors of two types will
                             emerge.
                             *Temporary Professor - will be
                             under a contract for a certain
                             number of years.
                             *Permanent Professor- will have
                             a regular, full, permanent
                             position.

Kindergarten Up-Date

     The Expert Committee for National Education, has
recommended kindergarten become compulsory so students
would receive a better start in education. Solidarity
and church leaders objected to this proposal. The
State would have control over children and might limit
connection between parent and child. Kindergartens are
voluntary exept for children who are age six and are in
zero class. Kindergartens are then compulsory.

     Some parents, due to the rising costs of kinder-
garten education, are now choosing not to send their
children to school. As a result, buildings are closing
and teachers are no longer needed.

AIDS

     Early programs which helped treat drug users now
now include HIV or AIDS victims.

     MONAR is one organization or movement set up to
help drug and AIDS victims. They organized care centers in Warsaw, but neighborhood people were very much
against having these centers. Fights erupted between
the center organizers, neighborhood people, and the
police. In many instances the people won and centers
did not open. Now there is very strong social opposition to the centers.

     AIDS victims are in abundance on the streets
asking for money and help. There is a lack of knowledge about the problem and fairy tales persist. There
remains no social programs to help these people, and
unfortunately, no one seems to care.

     One tiny light in this matter comes from the
educational people. School personnel attended a seminar which dealt with AIDS. They were given help in how
to talk with children about the AIDS condition. In

addition, they received help in dispelling some popular
opinions about AIDS. The teacher who attended the
seminar liked the quality of information she received.
However, she felt a need to have open-minded people
handle the situation. Some older staff members felt
very uncomfortable and ashamed to use many terms, such
as condom.

Teacher Shortages

     Poland, a country in transition, no longer has a
shortage of teachers. Still other people will say yes
Poland does have a shortage of qualified teachers. The
issue is, what type and kind of teachers are we talking
about?

     On one point, no one in Poland will debate. There
is a shortage of language teachers especially English,
German, and French. Changes in the school curriculum
require students to study, as soon as possible, a
Western language. (See section on Foreign Language
Teachers Needed in Chapter 9).

     Some people feel there is no longer a teacher
shortage. Many people who received training as teachers
instead became party officials. Therefore, many political, governmental, industrial, and social organizations absorbed the teacher candidates. With the change
in government, many of these former Communists became
unwanted people. This phenomenon was painfully true in
the many small villages and towns across Poland. Now
they want back into the teaching ranks. Some feel that
the present government should allow them back as teachers. However, unemployment is a current problem in
Poland. People feel if the former party officials are
unable to return to employment, they may become des-
peradoes.

     Another argument is that due to unemployment, many
graduating students from the universities during the
1990's will not be able to find teaching jobs.

     Teachers will not be scarce in urban areas and
larger cities, but there exists and will exist a lack
of teachers for rural Poland. Unfortunately, the
poorer qualified candidates find their way to the
hinterlands.

     Many Poles feel that the past totalitarian state
people should not return as teachers. They are not
happy with the prospect of these people who embraced

the ideology of the Socialist regime or their mentality. They simply do not fit the present educational
model.   Another fact is that for many years these
people have not been in a classroom with students and
therefore, teaching skills have diminished or disap-
peared.   Further, many are of an older generation and
might experience deep psychological difficulties when
suddenly immersed in a classroom of young Poles.

     Due to joblessness and a very poor economy, former
teachers are winding their way back into the profession.   This is understandable because in previous years
these positions carried high salaries, but now their
number has declined.   Notable examples have occurred
in industries such as newspaper and publishing houses.

     Therefore, a teacher is relatively secure and the
position is more attractive.

Private (Social) Schools

     Parents in local communities may set up and manage
private, social schools called Szkola Spotezna. Iza-
belle Kalińska (personal interview, 30 September 1990)
One local community near Warsaw, had ten days in which
to prepare the new school.   These schools follow the
basic curriculum from the State, but with changes.   One
change is a requirement of five hours of a western
foreign language per week.   Now two classes of English,
one class of French, and one class of German may be
chosen by the students.   Many parents will spend up to
three hundred thousand złotys per month, per child,
for extra tutoring in languages.   Further changes
include more gymnastics classes and the introduction of
computer classes in the future.   A student in grade
one, for example, would have classes in English, Polish, and mathematics. Other classes would include
drawing, music, technical and manual, gymnastics, and
environment.

     The curriculum of this community sponsored school
includes:

1st Grade -28 hours/week
Polish - 8 hrs   English or German - 4 hrs
Mathematics - 5 hrs   Arts - 2 hrs
Music - 2 hrs   Environment - 1 hr
Workshop - 2 hrs   Physical Educ. - 3 hrs
Religion - 1 hr

2nd <u>Grade</u> - <u>29</u> hours/week
Polish - 8 hrs   Mathematics - 5 hrs
English or German - 4 hrs   Physical Educ. - 2 hrs
Arts - 2 hrs   Music - 2 hrs
Workshop - 2 hrs   Environment - 2 hrs
Religion - 2 hrs

3rd <u>Grade</u> - <u>29</u> hours/week
Polish - 7 hrs   Mathematics - 5 hrs
English or German - 5 hrs   Physical Educ. - 3 hrs
Arts - 2 hrs   Music - 2 hrs
Workshop - 2 hrs   Environment - 2 hrs
Religion - 1 hr

4th <u>Grade</u> - <u>30</u> hours/week
Polish - 7 hrs   Mathematics - 5 hrs
English or German - 4 hrs   Physical Educ. - 3 hrs
Arts - 1 hr   Music - 1 hr
Workshop - 2 hrs   Biology - 2 hrs
Geography - 2 hrs   History - 1 hr
Religion - 1 hr

Schoolmaster's Hour - 1

The one hundred and twenty students come from a one to one and one half mile radius of the school, to an old military barracks. The Institute for Ecology bus transports students to and from school. The cost is 20,000 złotys per child per month. This year it is possible to attend classes for zero through grade four with plans to add additional grades next year. Hours of operation are from 8:00 a.m. to 4:00 p.m. with classes scheduled up to 12:30 or 1:30 p.m. Students may stay at the school until closing if they wish. An important feature is holding class enrollment to sixteen students per class. Low enrollment contrasts to one state school in the area with such a high enrollment that three or four shifts are necessary per day.

Homework is not necessary for students in grades zero to three. In fact, teachers sign a contract to have students complete all work at school. Teachers teach and students do all work at school. Students who may not be passing or doing good work can take additional classes.

Financial concerns were prevalent during the first year of operation. Each parent paid two hundred thousand złotys for start up funds. The town council provided some funds to change an old military barracks into the school. The cost per child per month is

three hundred thousand zlotys. A foundation raised
funds for expenses along with the National government
providing fifty per cent of the funds. The main prem-
ise is that a child should have the right to an education, therefore monies are distributed from the National government.

Parents, teachers, and local business people
helped by painting, decorating, fixing and building
school furniture, and other items necessary to start a
school.

The Director of the school faced many problems.
However, by sheer force of his determination, the
school became a reality. Teachers receive a salary
slightly higher than the normal salary of teachers in
the State system.

Parents and students alike love the school. They
support the changes in the curriculum, teacher attitudes and the general operations. Private schools are
an attractive alternative to schools of the Communist
period.

CHAPTER 10

CONCLUSIONS

1989 Conclusions - Before Change in Government

1. Tremendous teacher shortages especially in kindergarten and foreign languages.

2. Teachers allowed to leave a school job during the year for a better position.

3. No classes in computers for students in school.

4. Poorly prepared teachers due to a lack of qualified teacher training programs.

5. Teacher training programs do not include courses designed to provide teaching strategies and methods.

6. State run schools, curriculum, and texts.

7. Little opportunity for private schools.

8. Lack of adequate physical facilities.

9. Lack of teaching materials.

10. Heavy reliance on lecture method of instruction.

11. Compulsory attendance for only nine years.

12. Quality of classroom interaction. Student vs. teacher and teacher vs. student attitudes prevailed.

13. Instructional time not properly used. Student absences, teacher absences, problem of keeping time-on-task for student.

14. No student evaluations of teachers and courses.

15. Official educational data is often misleading.

16. High dropout rate of students at University level.

17. No coordination between various levels of educa-
     tion.

1990-91 Conclusions - After Change in Government

1.   Ministry of Education personnel favor keeping the
     current educational system, but allowing change to
     occur from the bottom up. The old system is
     impossible to fix, therefore, any real educational
     reform must start at the bottom.

2.   Headmasters and teachers have the power to make
     changes at the local school level. Teachers now
     have the decision-making power in their class-
     rooms, determine teaching strategies, use varied
     classroom procedures, and write new classroom
     materials.

3.   New materials for classroom use continue to be
     scarce. Teachers are writing new materials, but
     lack of paper and excessively long production
     times remain as problems.

4.   Private schools, called social schools, may legal-
     ly operate in Poland. Their numbers are rapidly
     increasing. Local parents or private companies
     usually set up these new schools. Characteristics
     include a high tuition cost, teach regular school
     curriculum, and offer additional classes in for-
     eign languages, problem solving, and business.
     The schools usually have a low student enrollment.

5.   University curricula changed to model United
     States' universities.

6   New system of academic ranks and titles exist at
     the University level.

7.   All students must take a western foreign language
     and the process should start in grade one, if
     possible.

8.   New three-year English teachers colleges now train
     candidates as a shortage of qualified language

teachers exist.   They will receive the B.A. degree,
with no thesis required.

9.   Programs exist in the wider culture for treatment
of AIDS victims.   School personnel are slowly developing similar programs.

10.   Teaching religion in the schools is now possible.

11.   Former military barracks have been converted to
      use for schools.

12.   Teacher shortages still exist in rural Poland.
      Urban and large cities no longer are experiencing
      dire teacher shortages.

STOPIEŃ	grade
KOŃCZYĆ SZKOLE	graduate
SZKOŁA	school
SZKOŁA PODSTAWOWA	primary school
SZKOŁA ŚREDINA	secondary school
PRZEDSZKOŁE	nursery school
KURATOR/INSPEKTOR	superintendent
UNIWERSYTET	university
NAUCZYCIEL	teacher
PROGRAM	curriculum
KURS	course
UCZEŃ	pupil
DYPLOM	diploma
ŚWIADECTWO	certificate
ZERÓWKA	pre-schools
SZKOŁA SPOŁECZNA	social schools

Adamowicz, Ala. Personal Interview, 16 May 1989.

An Outline History of Polish Culture. Jagiellonian
    University, Interpress Publishers, Warszawa, 1984.

Dakowski, Maria. Personal Interview, 16 April 1989.

Davies, Norman. Heart of Europe: A Short History of
    Poland. Oxford University Press, Oxford, 1989.

Doktor, Tadeusz. "Outside Catholicism - The
    Enlightened Path," The Warsaw Voice, 8 May 1989.

Edukacja Narodowym Priorytetem, Państowe Wydawnictwo
    Naukowe, Warszawa-Kraków, 1989.

Falkowska, Bozenna.   Personal Interview, 16 April
    1989.

Kalińska, Isabelle. Personal Interview, 30 September
    1990.

Kolendo M., Zoziejow tajnego nauczania w latach oku-
    pacji: 1941-44. Białstok, 1966.

Kruszewski, Krzsztof, Dr. Personal Interview, 29 March
    1989.

Kupisiewicz, Czesław. Personal Interview. 21 April
    1989.

Miaso, Józef, Historia Wychowania, Panstwowe Wydaw-
    nictwo Naukowe, Warszawa, 1980.

Michener, James A. Iberia. Fawcett, New York, 1988.

Ministry of National Education of the Polish People's
    Republic. Development of Education Within 1986-
    1988. Report for the International Education
    Office in Geneva for the 41st. Session of the
    International Education Conference, Warsaw, 1988.

Sokolewicz, Zofia Blanka. Personal Interview, 4 May
    1989.

Statistical Yearbook, Warsaw, 1988.

Świecki, Andrzej. Poland A Handbook. Interpress
    Publishers. Warsaw, 1977.

The International Encyclopedia of Education, Volume 7,
    Pergamon Press, Oxford, 1985. pp. 3951-3955.

Welbel, Stefan and Jola. Personal Interview. 24 April
    1989.

102 WORKS CITED

Zaciura, Jan Dr. Personal Interview, 25 April 1989.

Zawada, Bonita. Class Interview. 1989.

Zuk, Andrzej. Class Interview. 1989.

Index

changing positions about, 86
governmental leaders position about, 86
non-believers wishes about, 86
other religious groups wishes about, 86
Roman Catholic Church position about, 86
Technical High School in Białystok, 37-39
  curriculum offered in, 37-38
  dormitories for, 37
  examination of students in, 38
  lack of physical space in, 38-39
  staff members in, 37
  teachers in, 39

universities, 40-41
University of Wilna, 8
  see also Russian Partition Sector, 8
university student organizations, 85
  active role taken by, 85
  Niezalegny Zwiozek Studentów, 85
  Zrzeszenie Studentów Polskich, 85

weaknesses of Polish education, 59-60

Zero Class, 27
  see also kindergartens - school #77, Białystok, 27
Zrzeszenie Studentów Polskich, 85
  see also university student organizations, 85